The Art of Bead Embroidery

KALMBACH BOOKS

The Art of Bead Embroidery

Technique, Design, & Inspiration

Heidi Kummli
Sherry Serafini

Kalmbach Books

21027 Crossroads Circle

Waukesha, Wisconsin 53186

www.Kalmbach.com/Books

Printed in the United States of America

13 12 11 10 09   3 4 5 6 7

Publisher's Cataloging-in-Publication Data

Serafini, Sherry.
  The art of bead embroidery : technique, design, and inspiration / by Sherry Serafini and Heidi Kummli.

  p. : ill. ; cm.

  Includes bibliographical references.
  ISBN: 978-0-87116-243-4

1. Bead embroidery. 2. Embroidery. 3. Beadwork. I. Kummli, Heidi. II. Title.

NK9302 .S47 2007
746.5

Foreword

"Everything on the surface seems to move. I see circles, spirals, and loops. And symmetry."

The first time I saw the photo of Sherry Serafini's beadwork on the cover of *Bead&Button* magazine in 2003, I was transfixed and unable to put the page down. I went to clean the sink and kept going back to study the beadwork. I finally went to the copy store and made color copies so I could have the image with me — in my studio, in my car, and over the sink. How was this type of work done? Would I ever be able to bead with such majestic stitches? I need a book!

A few weeks later, a friend told me about Heidi Kummli's piece that won first place in the bead category of the Saul Bell Design Awards, and I went to her Web site to see her work. Her pieces are at once ethereal and emotional. I was delighted to find that she lives a short distance from me and soon thereafter, we met when she was a guest artist in a bead store. I saw her beautiful beaded jewelry and bags and once more, I was mesmerized. I returned several times to study these lovely pieces during the evening and left feeling inspired and excited. It's difficult to sleep when you see that kind of beaded art.

Although I had done some bead embroidery, I had not seen embroidery techniques, charms, and cabochons used in this way. I am fascinated by tiny seed beads (that was back when I thought 11°s were tiny) and had started to use them in my own work. But seeing Sherry and Heidi's works of art gave new meaning to those tiny bits of glass.

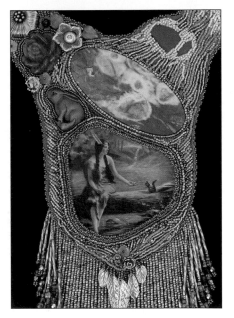

Like most bead artists, I was curious and fascinated and wanted to learn more about bead embroidery methods. What foundations and glues would one use? Where does one start, or for that matter, finish? And, I wondered where to find such unusual materials to incorporate into a beaded piece.

The Art of Bead Embroidery: Technique, Design, and Inspiration will answer these questions and more. You will be inspired by these two very talented and prolific women: one who works in an upstairs space high in the Rocky Mountains and the other who works in her kitchen near a big city in Pennsylvania.

Both artists are surrounded with the sights and sounds of the real world: family, kids, pets, confusion, and even chaos at times. But it doesn't slow down their art life. In that way they are centered and profound.

No matter where we are or what our circumstances, to bead is a solitary activity for the most part. It's fun to bead with our friends, but the real discovery happens as we sit with the beads, placing them one at a time on the needle and watching that idea form and become something seductive and poetic.

Why couldn't I have had a book like this to do a book report on at school? I'll look at this book many times and read it from cover to cover. Sherry and Heidi have given us a complete, no secrets allowed, lovely-to-gaze-upon book.

May you feel the thrill of inspiration as I have.

—Janet Kay Skeen

Janet Kay Skeen, dba *Janet from Another Planet*, has shown her work in the Interweave traveling shows *The Beaded Cloth* and *The Beaded Figure*. She had two pieces in Bead International 2006. Janet has written articles and lectured about beadwork throughout the United States. She lives in Denver where she beads most days, teaches beadwork, is active in the Rocky Mountain Bead Society, paints a bit, and has tea with friends as often as possible.

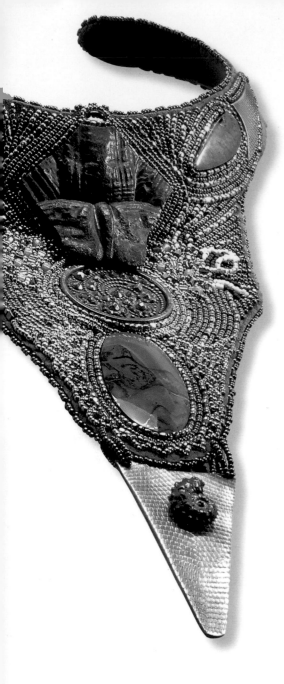

Contents

Sherry

I t's 4 a.m. and the lights go on in a home outside the city of Pittsburgh. I begin my day. Believing that there aren't enough hours in a day to do everything I want to do, I like to start early to get as much out of my time as possible. My large, naturally lit kitchen is my studio; it comes alive with a can of Mountain Dew, the preparation of dinner for later, feeding the dogs, a new beading project, and the sounds of Aerosmith coming from the stereo.

Unusual objects and shapes become part of a new story as I stitch beads and gemstones, one at a time, to a suede base. Most pieces are born spontaneously as the beads and my imagination dictate the design. I seldom work from sketches. I find this meditative art form to be a rich counterpoint to a society full of instant gratification.

I was raised in a military family, moving every few years. I credit that nomadic lifestyle with giving me an adventurous spirit and uninhibited approach to my artwork.

My mother once said, "Sherry was born with a crayon in her hand!" I was always the kid who would rather paint or play with clay than go out at recess and run around the playground. To get through art school, I freelanced as a graphic designer, doing portraits, painting signs, and lettering on race cars. From childhood to adulthood, I loved the arts, but seemed to be searching for the one true art form that I felt defined my soul.

I graduated with a graphic design degree from the Art Institute of Pittsburgh in 1987. I then married Greg and found work as an ad director for a local newspaper. However, it wasn't until the birth of my first daughter, Erika, in 1991 that I started to dabble in beads. Choosing to stay home with my new daughter, I quit my work in the ad department.

Beading became a full-time career in 1997. It is the only medium I have remained true to and see no end in my love for beaded artwork. I am primarily self-taught. My work has won many competitions, is represented by major beading companies, and has been used by the legendary rock band Aerosmith both as adornment and in promotional material.

I firmly believe that our lives and talents are a gift from God. I hope that my beaded artwork inspires and touches the lives of others.

I live just outside Pittsburgh, Pennsylvania on 12 acres of land that I share with my husband Greg, daughters Erika and Nikki, and our two dogs, Abby and Lucy.

Heidi

M y soul is the mountains with snow blankets on them.
My soul is an open plain in the desert.
My soul is every living thing!
—By Benjamin August Nakai Tarantino (Heidi's son)

As you wander off the scenic highway outside Ward, Colorado, you'll head down a dirt road blessed with potholes and ruts: nature's speed bumps. Finally, you come around the last bend in the road and before you is an awesome view of the Indian Peaks Wilderness that will blow you away if the wind doesn't.

To the right, nestled on the mountainside, is my family's home. "Big Blue," the plow truck, will welcome you up the drive along with old metal cans and artifacts from yesteryear. On the inside, I surround myself with Indian prints, antiques, and artwork traded from years of doing art shows. My studio on the top floor greets me every morning with natural light and mountain views shining through the windows.

Though I have been beading since 1980, it became a full-time job in 1990 when I quit my real job of eight years gluing crystal figurines. I remember as a child making jewelry out of found objects, such as pop-can tabs and pinecones. My great grandmother was a Chippewa Indian and did beadwork for Vaudeville. My grandfather was a magnificent wood carver, a talent my mother also acquired. When my father was 23, he came to the United States from Switzerland. He didn't speak the language but taught himself to be a success-ful mechanical engineer.

With all these traits flowing through me, how could I not be creative? I have taught myself all my beading techniques, learning from books and trial and error. My work has been published in several books and I have won numerous awards throughout my career. The most memorable was in 2003 when I won first place at the Saul Bell Awards for beadwork, and where I met Sherry. We became instant friends; sisters of the bead. I enjoy competitions because it keeps me on my toes and keeps me humble.

My husband Gregg, son Ben, and I live on 12 acres totally off the grid. We have two dogs and two cats and lots of fresh air at 8,900 feet above sea level. I believe by living with and respecting the earth as one, we are one. I hope to share the beauty of my surroundings through my work and spread peace and calmness to those I touch along the way.

Heidi F Kummli

Authors' Note

As we worked on this book together, we discovered a lot about one another as well as about ourselves. We read about one another's stitches, foundations, and glues. We laughed at how similar or different they were. How is it possible that two women who live hundreds of miles apart, have only met twice, and are totally self-taught can have the same techniques yet be so different?

We hope that you will find this book easy to use, fun, and inspirational, and that it will answer many of your bead embroidery questions. We review the stitches we both use and our favorite tools, including some you can make at home. We explore our design philosophy with photographs to inspire and challenge you. You will learn about the best foundations, linings, backings, and glues to use for bead embroidery. We teach you how to finish your beadwork — which for both of us is pretty much the same — and how to add fringe — where we are completely different.

We each have six projects. You'll begin with a simple project and work your way up to a complex collar. We've picked projects that let you use all the stitches and techniques in this book. You'll learn as you work your way through them, you will laugh, you will swear, but in the end, you will smile.

Our projects are given to you for your own personal enjoyment, for you to learn, grow, and maybe share as a gift. We both make a living from our art, so please don't mass-produce or teach these projects. Our goal in writing this book together is to share our knowledge with you, so that you can feel confident in your heart to create with passion and individuality.

We hope to have opened the door to your minds and inspired you to create. Learning from others is what we all do, but what is unique is making it your own.

—Sherry Serafini and Heidi Kummli

Facts

- Sherry and Heidi both live on 12 acres of land, walk their two dogs each day, have a child the same age, love to do beadwork, and have husbands with the name Greg or Gregg.

- Both artists won People's Choice awards at the Bead Dreams competition (Heidi in 2005 and Sherry in 2006).

- Heidi and Sherry spend about 20 percent of the day playing door monitor for their dogs.

- Heidi and Sherry both go through about 3,500 grams of seed beads a year. And, each can consume approximately 500 grams of chocolate a year.

- Sherry and Heidi have met only twice; they first met in 2003 at the Saul Bell awards. But they are soul sisters connected in some strange way. Coincidence? They don't think so; it was meant to be.

- Heidi and Sherry encourage you to get inspired by others but create from your heart.

Here's an introduction to the tools we use daily, easy embroidery stitches, the best foundation, lining, and backing for your work, our favorite adhesives, and finally, finishing and fringe. Begin with these techniques, and then add a few of your own. Never stop being challenged.

chnique

TOOLS

I t was — and still is — the simplicity of the tools that continues to draw us to create with beads. For beadwork it doesn't take many: a needle, some thread, and you're good to go. It doesn't take a lot of room to do beadwork either. Below is a list of tools we use on a daily basis; many of them can be made from household items. These tools will help make beading more pleasurable for you, but by all means are not mandatory.

Tools by Sherry and Heidi

Beads

It all begins with the beads. We like to use all kinds of seed beads, from the tiniest size 15°s to the bigger and bolder 8°s. Bugles add linear elements to our designs and are perfect for fringe. Pearls, crystals, glass beads, and gemstones enhance any beadwork. Cabochons often are our starting point for color and for design. Let your imagination inspire you as you select your beads.

Bead board

The bead board is handy for any kind of beading. It's a piece of cardboard covered with fabric; you can then spread your beads out and they won't roll all over. If you have several bead boards, you can lay out different projects on the boards and stack them, if you wish.

Make your own bead board by cutting a piece of cardboard into a 12 x 8-in. (30 x 20cm) rectangle. This measurement works well because if you're stringing a 24-in. (61cm) necklace, you know where the middle of the necklace will be because your bead board is 12 in. long. This works the same for a 16-in. (41cm) necklace in the opposite direction. Cover the cardboard with Ultrasuede or another low-fiber fabric so your needle won't catch. Don't choose a fabric that's too smooth, or your beads will move too much, which defeats the purpose. Neutral colors work best, such as grays and beiges. Cut your fabric about 1½ in. (3.8cm) larger than the cardboard, and using masking tape, adhere it to the back side of your cardboard nice and snug. You now have a great work surface for your beading projects. You can stick your needles directly in the board for easy access.

Beading wire

Use wire, such as Beadalon .021 or .019 for stringing necklace strands. Sherry also uses 6- or 8-lb. Fireline. Finish the ends with crimps.

Clothespins

Clothespins are great clamps. Use them to hold down an odd-shaped cabochon or button while the glue is drying. You also can use them to clamp your finished beadwork to a curved bracelet. You will find many other uses for clothespins.

Compass

Use a compass to measure the inner circle of collar projects.

Cotton swabs

Use cotton swabs and a little water for cleaning up your beadwork and Ultrasuede after your project is complete.

TOOLS

Hole Reamer

Crimper

Of course you will use your crimper for the crimp beads at the ends of your necklaces, but this little tool is great to eliminate a bead you don't want in a place that's hard to get to (just crush the bead with the pliers' jaws). Make sure you close your eyes when destroying unwanted beads — the glass will fly.

Emery board or metal files

Use a metal file for filing off the backs of metal buttons or other sharp objects. Emery boards work great for roughing up the back of a smooth cabochon or polymer-clay piece before gluing.

Fine-point marker

Use a marker to draw designs (if desired) and for tracing patterns onto Lacy's Stiff Stuff or Ultrasuede. If it's nonpermanent, you can clean up the marker line later.

Hole reamer

The hole reamer is a handmade tool for putting holes in things. When you're finishing a pair of post earrings, the hole reamer helps you put the hole in the Ultrasuede so your post goes through easily. You also can use it to put holes in your earring display cards. It's handy for taking out knots as well.

To make the hole reamer, glue an embroidery needle into a cork. It's that easy.

Lighter

Use a lighter for burning off short ends of thread.

Needlenose pliers

Needlenose pliers are used not only for bending wire but also for pulling needles through tough beads or Ultrasuede.

Needles

Heidi uses size #12 sharps for bead embroidery and #12 longs for fringe. Sherry uses #10, #12, and #13 longs for everything.

Patterns

Make your own collar-necklace patterns by cutting old shirts and using the collar as your pattern. Transfer the shape onto poster board. (See p. 66 and p. 92 for Sherry's and Heidi's collar projects for more tips.) You can also make patterns from poster board for cuff bracelets so you know the exact size to cut your Ultrasuede.

Scoop pattern

tape or glue tab to back

folds

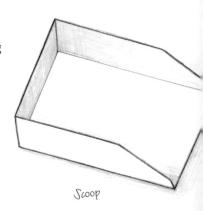

Scoop

Ruler

Use a ruler for making straight lines on a collar project or for measuring various patterns. You've got to have straight lines!

Scissors

Scissors will become your best friend. Cute little scissors are just that — cute. You need scissors with long, strong blades. You will be using your scissors to cut off excess Ultrasuede and other foundations from your beadwork, and often using the tips, so they must be strong and sharp. You don't need to spend a lot of money on them as they usually need to be replaced once a year.

Scoop

The scoop is another must for beaders. Use this handy tool to scoop up extra beads and return them to their tiny little bags and vials. It's also great for scooping up the threads that end up all over your work space. To make a scoop, enlarge the pattern by 200%. Trace it onto an old cereal box or heavy paper and cut it out. Fold on the dotted lines (for heavy paper, score the line with a ruler and a utility knife so it folds better), then tape or glue the tabs in place.

Scrap paper

Cut up small pieces of scrap paper for mixing glue. It's nice to have a pile ready to go.

Thread

Heidi uses Nymo B in black or beige depending on the Ultrasuede color. Sherry uses Nymo B and D in either black or white. Thread color can change the look of your beads if the beads are transparent, as the thread will show.

Toothpicks and craft sticks

Use for spreading and mixing glue. See more about gluing on pp. 26 and 27.

Utility knife

Use a utility knife to cut Ultrasuede when preparing a pin back or barrette. It also comes in handy for cleaning up excess glue if you did a sloppy glue job.

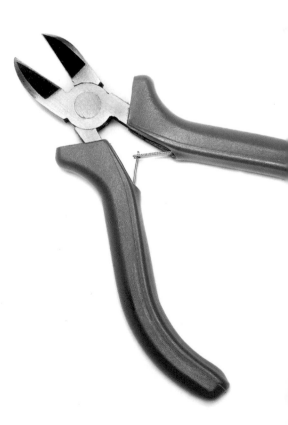

White paper

You'll need paper for sketching designs and using as a template.

Wire cutters

Wire cutters are used for cutting off the backs of metal buttons or other metal objects that need to be altered.

STITCHES

There are many published bead embroidery stitches, but we only use about five or six very basic stitches in our work. "Keep it simple, stupid" as an old friend used to say; funny, maybe, but that's a great motto. By using fewer stitches, you can perfect the ones you do use. Be creative and make up your own. The stitches we use may be familiar to you, or maybe you know them by a different name. We've used the names that we're used to, and these names are used throughout the book. For example, Heidi's Basic Edging and Sherry's Picot Brick Stitch are very similar; the number of beads are the only difference. Most of these directions assume you are beading on a foundation such as Lacy's Stiff Stuff or Ultrasuede.

Sherry's Stitches

Photo by Larry Sanders

Backstitch 2

Backstitch 2 is the stitch I use for all of my backgrounds. Because of the many curves in my beaded patterns, I've found stitching two at a time is best for me to keep my beads flat against the foundation. I use it for going around cabochons, buttons, and for creating paths with seed beads in patterned work.

Cut a 2-ft. (61cm) length of thread and add a #12 or #13 beading needle. Knot the end. Pass your needle up through the foundation next to a stone or wherever you want to start. Add two beads and pull them down to the foundation, laying them in the direction you want them to go. Pass your needle down through the foundation next to where the second bead rests, pulling all the thread and beads down tight to the foundation. Then pass the needle back up from the underside of the beadwork where your first bead is strung. Pass your needle through the beads one more time, exiting the second bead. String on two more beads and pass the needle down through the foundation against the fourth bead. Come back up between the first and second beads, pass through the second, third, and fourth beads again, and string on two more beads. Continue on in this manner.

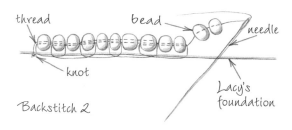

Backstitch 2

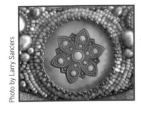

Photo by Larry Sanders

Even-count peyote stitch

Even-count peyote stitch is used to capture cabochons. To do this, bring your needle straight up from underneath the foundation and position it between two beads in your backstitched round. Pass the needle through one seed bead. String a seed bead on the needle, skip the next bead in the base round, and pass the needle through the following bead. You are essentially skipping every other bead. Repeat around until you are at your starting position. If you have backstitched around a cabochon or button, keep an even number of beads to allow for even-count peyote.

Since you started with an even number of beads on your backstitched base round, you will now need to step-up to continue: Now that you've gone all the way around your cabochon and you're back to the first bead you added, you will go through it again to begin the next round. This is called the step-up.

You can tell when you get to the end of a round as there seems to be no place to add a new bead. But if you go back through the bead where you began and the first bead of the round just stitched, you will find you can now add a bead. You have stepped-up into the next round. Pick up a bead, pass the needle through the bead beside it and continue around in this manner, stepping up when you get to the end of each round. Note: You are only going through two beads in the step-up.

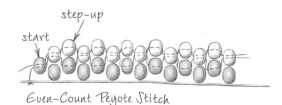

Even-Count Peyote Stitch

STITCHES

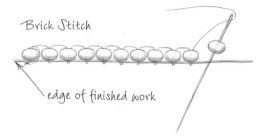

Brick Stitch

edge of finished work

Photo by Larry Sanders

Brick stitch

I use brick stitch along the edges of my beadwork to finish the piece. This is often referred to as edging. To edge, thread a needle with a 1-yd. (.9m) single-strand length of beading thread and knot the end. Sew into the beadwork at the edge to anchor the thread. With the needle exiting the top edge of the beadwork, pick up an 11° or 14° bead and sew up through the foundation and the Ultrasuede to attach. Before tightening the stitch, sew up through the bead. The bead will stand out from the edge of the piece. Pick up another 11° and sew down through the foundation, Ultrasuede, and then back up and exit the top of the bead. Continue around the entire piece, sewing through the edge of the beadwork and the edge of the Ultrasuede. The idea is to seam the two pieces together. When you've edged the entire way around your work, and your last bead meets the first bead you sewed on, go down through the first bead to join the two. Pass your needle through some beads on your beadwork, making several small knots in the beadwork and hiding them in the beads. Clip the thread as close to the beadwork as you can. Be careful not to cut the beadwork.

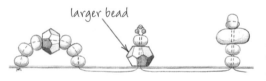

larger bead

Stop Stitches for pearls and odd shapes

Photo by Larry Sanders

Stop stitches for pearls and odd shapes

When stitching large beads or pearls, I like to use a stitch that I call stop stitch.

Pass the needle up from underneath the foundation material. Pick up a larger bead, perhaps a 6° or a pearl. Pull the bead tight against the foundation. Add a 14° or 11° seed bead, skip the bead just strung, pass the needle back down through the larger bead and through the foundation. Pull tightly to secure the large bead. Repeat this process to make sure the bead does not "bobble" around on the foundation.

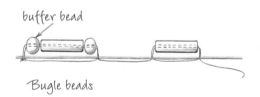

buffer bead

Bugle beads

Bugle beads

Sew on bugle beads (or any long, narrow beads) one at a time, and always sew through them twice, as they can be sharp. You may even consider a "buffer" bead at either end of the bugle to protect the thread from potentially sharp edges; just stitch a seed bead at each end of the bugle bead.

Photo by Larry Sanders

Crystals and other faceted beads

Sew crystals so one of the facets lies against the foundation. Crystals also can be sewn on top of the finished beadwork as an eye-catching embellishment. Size 4mm crystals look great when treated as a seed bead and sewn on with Backstitch 2 to surround a cabochon or focal point within the design.

Picot brick stitch

Similar to simple brick stitch, but instead of stitching one bead at a time, you will create a picot edge as you go around the piece. Pick up three seed beads. Measure about one seed bead over from the thread and sew down through the Lacy's and the Ultrasuede. Sew back up through the Lacy's, the Ultrasuede, and the third seed bead. Pull snug. Next, add two seed beads and sew down through the Lacy's and Ultrasuede, and pass the needle back up through the Lacy's, Ultrasuede, and second seed bead strung. Continue around in this manner. This is especially nice on cuffs, earrings, or brooches that you do not plan to fringe.

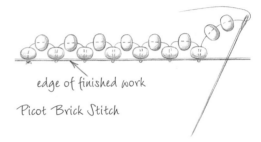

edge of finished work

Picot Brick Stitch

Heidi's Stitches

Backstitch 4

Backstitch 4 is a really simple stitch you can use for all kinds of applications. It's great for going around small cabochons or doing small detail work. Push a threaded needle up through your foundation next to a stone or wherever you want to start. Pick up four beads and pull them down to the Ultrasuede, laying them in the direction you want them to go — this could be next to a stone, following a straight line, or wherever your path leads you. Now push your needle down through the Ultrasuede next to where the fourth bead rests, pulling all the thread and beads down tight to the Ultrasuede. With your needle, go back up between the second and third bead and push your needle and thread through the last two beads. Add another four beads and repeat the process as far as you need to go. After you have gone around the cabochon or finished your round, make sure to go back through all the beads again — this pulls the beads together nicely and also straightens the round. Add as many rounds as you wish. When adding additional rounds, make sure not to start them too close to the first or they will bunch up and not lie flat.

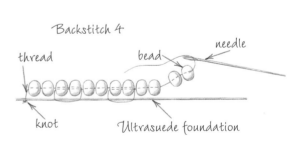

Backstitch 4

thread

bead

needle

knot

Ultrasuede foundation

STITCHES

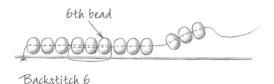

Backstitch 6

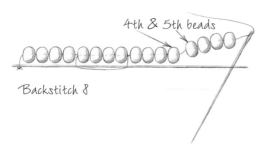

Backstitch 8

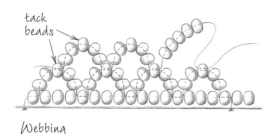

Webbing

Backstitch 6

Backstitch 6 is great for beading around larger cabochons and beading lines. The only difference between Backstitch 4 and 6 is the number of beads you start with. For Backstitch 6 you will be adding six beads to start, and going back up through the third and fourth bead and the last three beads. As in Backstitch 4, always make sure to sew back through each round.

Backstitch 8

Use Backstitch 8 for beading around large cabochons, or beading long straight lines. Again, the only difference between Backstitch 4, 6, and 8 is the number of beads you start with and go back through. With Backstitch 8, you begin with eight beads and go back through the fourth and fifth bead and the last three beads. As before, make sure you sew back through the round of beads again. This is most important in Backstitch 8, as it really helps pull the beads together.

Webbing

Webbing is great for beading up the side of a tall cabochon or button. By simply using tack beads, you also can use webbing on your foundation for a unique lacy look in your work.

For beading up the side of a cabochon, sew the first round of beads using Backstitch 4 or 6. Exit through a bead and add an odd number of beads (three or five) so you have a middle bead to tack with or to add another round to. To add five beads (as in the drawing) skip three beads on the initial round and sew into the fourth bead. Continue adding five beads at a time around the stone and round of beads. You may need to adjust the number of beads as you work your way around to the first five-bead set. Now bring your needle up through the third (or middle) bead of the first five-bead set. Again you can add three or five beads here. If this is going to be your final round, I recommend adding only three beads as this will bring your beadwork nice and tight to the sides of the stone. Repeat around as desired. Go through the last round again to pull everything nice and snug against the stone and straighten the beads. If you want to continue the rounds of webbing, you can continue as before. By adding and subtracting beads, you can go around unusual cabochons and shapes. Be creative here.

If you are webbing flat on the foundation, use the same process as above, but tack the center bead of each stitch down to the foundation. Pick up the five beads for the first stitch and lay them on the foundation where desired. Sew down through the foundation, come up next to the tack bead, sew through the tack bead, and go down and up through the foundation on the other side of the bead. Continue to tack the rest of the stitches in the same way. As mentioned, you can add as many rounds as you wish, or change the number of beads you use to make different patterns. Since you're always tacking the middle bead down before you start your next stitch, you don't need to go back through all the beads as you do on the other stitches.

Snaking stitch

The snaking stitch is very much like the webbing stitch. The only difference is you add beads inside the webbing to give it more of a scaly look: hence the name *snake*. You will need to start with a round of beads. I prefer to use a larger bead, such as a 9º, for the first round and then use a 15º for the actual webbing. It's best to use an odd number of beads — anywhere from three to five beads is good. Keep in mind that three beads won't allow you much room for adding the snake bead, but will work well for shaping the pattern where you wish.

Start by coming out one of the 9ºs on the initial round, add five 15ºs, skip two 9ºs, and sew through the next 9º. Continue adding webbing as desired. Go back and tack down your tack beads to the foundation (the tack bead is the third 15º, or middle bead). Now that you're tacked down, go through one of the third beads again and add another five 15º beads, and go through the next third bead (or tack bead) and repeat the process.

Once you have your desired pattern, you can add the snake beads. I like to use 9º beads in a color that will really stand out. With your needle and thread, come up through the foundation in a corner near the webbing and sew the bead in place; this is a fun process and very rewarding to watch your pattern grow. (You might need to use smaller-sized beads in places to prevent the webbing from buckling.)

Snaking Stitch

Simple edging

You can use this simple edging on all your projects. Once your project is glued and trimmed, you're ready for edging. Thread a #12 needle with a 2-ft. length of thread and knot one end. Push your needle between the foundation and the backing and bring it up through the top of the Ultrasuede about 1/16 in. (2mm) from the edge (this will hide the knot). Add four beads, pulling them down next to the Ultrasuede, and push your needle back up through the backing and foundation, about 1/8 in. (3mm) over from where you started. Sew back up through the fourth or last bead and pull the beads snug. Add three beads this time, positioning your needle about 1/8 in. from your last stitch and sewing back up through the last bead. Repeat this process along the edge, increasing or decreasing the number of beads in each stitch, as needed. Once you reach the starting point, add the required number of beads and go back down through the first bead strung and the backing. Tie a knot, and go through the backing about 1 in. (2.5cm) from the edge. Come out through the backing and cut the excess thread.

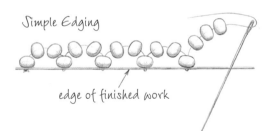

Simple Edging

edge of finished work

FOUNDATION/LINING/BACKING

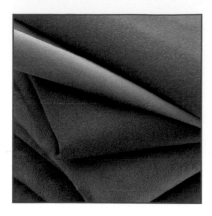

Ultrasuede is a synthetic suede and is available in many colors, so it's easy to match or complement your beadwork. Ultrasuede is strong, flexible, and doesn't fray when it's cut. It works as a lining or a backing.

Sherry's Foundation

My favorite foundation is Lacy's Stiff Stuff. It's a wonderful material that can be glued, painted, dyed, and drawn on. It also has unbelievable strength. It's very porous, which makes it great for gluing stones, because you'll only need to wait about 20 minutes for the stone to be secure. For beaders who prefer a stiffer embroidery surface, Lacy's is fabulous. I began my cabochon gluing "back in the day" on index cards and interfacing material. Since Lacy's Stiff Stuff came onto the market, I've been beading on it religiously. When working with certain colors, you may want to dye your Lacy's.

To dye: stir 1 tsp. powder dye to 2 cups boiling water. Watch carefully, as the dye will fizz and boil up. Allow the Lacy's to soak in the dye for 60 seconds. Rinse with cold water, and pat with a paper towel. Allow to air dry. Fabric paints or permanent markers also work great to color Lacy's.

Ultrasuede is another good beading foundation. It is a lightweight, synthetic version of suede and comes in a wide variety of colors. As opposed to Lacy's, it is a very flexible foundation.

Sherry's Lining

Cereal boxes and plastic container lids work great when you're embroidering a piece that requires added "stiffness." For example, a porcelain centerpiece or a long, heavier cabochon needs to be stabilized so the foundation won't bend. After beading the desired design, cut out the beadwork. Lay the beadwork down onto the plastic or stiff board and trace around the design. Cut out the piece you've traced, approximately $\frac{1}{16}$-in. (2mm) smaller than the beaded piece, as you will be edging and need to take the needle through the edges of the piece. Glue the plastic or cardboard to the back of the beadwork, and let dry. This lining becomes sandwiched between the beadwork and the backing.

Sherry's Backing

Ultrasuede is a wonderful backing. Ultrasuede is my preference as it is lightweight, which makes it easy to sew through when backstitching or doing a brick stitch edging technique. The many color choices make it easy to match the Ultrasuede to your beadwork.

If Ultrasuede is not available to you, leather or suede are good substitutes. But you will have to use a much stronger needle, as these materials are more difficult to stitch through.

Photo by Larry Sanders

Heidi's Foundation

You can use many fabrics for a foundation, but there are a few things you might want to consider.

The foundation's thickness is one; if it's thick, as leather is, you will need a stronger needle and a thimble. If your foundation is too thin, it may not give your beadwork the support it needs and it may be flimsy and hard to handle, especially if you're working with large stones.

The other consideration is fraying. When you cut the material, does it fray? If so, you don't want to use it for a foundation, unless it's already sewn (as in embroidering on a pair of jeans).

Ultrasuede is my ideal foundation material. You can cut it next to your beadwork and it won't fray. Ultrasuede is the perfect thickness for a #12 needle to pass through easily. It also comes in a large selection of colors, and is washable (not that you want to put your beadwork in the washing machine, but you can clean excess glue and marker off Ultrasuede with a wet cotton swab).

When you cut out your foundation, make sure you leave extra room; you never know if your design might grow as you bead. If you're using a pattern, trace it onto the Ultrasuede and then cut around the pattern leaving a 1-in. (2.5cm) border.

The Ultrasuede foundation used for this cuff becomes part of the design. And, because it's used on the back as well, it makes for a soft and comfortable fit.

Heidi's Lining

Your project determines the lining. In most cases, poster board works great. If you are making a bracelet, you'll need something flexible so you can curve it. Poster board is excellent for getting a curve and holding it. Fabric lining is another good lining for flexibility. You can get lining material at the fabric store in many different thicknesses; some are even thick enough for foundations and don't fray.

If, however, your project needs to stay flat because it has heavy stones, then you might need to use something thicker, such as a cereal box. You won't see the lining when the work is complete, so use something you already have around the house. Recycle those boxes!

To cut your lining, place the finished beadwork on top of the lining material and trace around the beadwork with a pencil. (If you use a pen, you might get ink on the Ultrasuede.) Cut the lining about ⅛-in. (3mm) smaller than the traced line or finished beadwork. Apply glue to the lining rather than the back of the beadwork — it's less messy this way. If you're working on a larger collar, it's a good idea to put glue on both sides. Now you're ready to apply the backing.

Heidi's Backing

The back of your piece is just as important as the front. Use Ultrasuede in the same color as your foundation. Lay the finished piece with the lining glued in place on the inside of the Ultrasuede, trace around the piece leaving ½-in. (1.3cm) extra Ultrasuede or more (don't cut yourself short here), and then cut. Spread the glue on the back of the lining and then lay it on the inside of the Ultrasuede just cut. Make sure you have extra Ultrasuede all the way around. Carefully press your beadwork into place, massaging it onto the backing. Now you're ready to begin the finishing, which will be covered on p. 28.

ADHESIVES

Adhesives have been around for over 6,000 years. The earliest evidence of humankind's adhesive use dates back to 4000 B.C. Archaeologists unearthed pots repaired with a tree-sap glue. Early glues also were made from egg white, blood, bones, milk, cheese, vegetables, tar, beeswax, sap, or animal hides. The industrial revolution accelerated advances in glue making, introducing new methods and ingredients.

Today there are many choices. Strength and flexibility are critical requirements for beadwork. Please read all the manufacturer's guidelines for safety and application. Our methods work for us but may vary for you depending on your climate or elevation. Experiment with your own glues to find what works best for you.

Photo by Larry Sanders

In beadwork and jewelry making, you need a strong glue to hold cabochons in place. A tip for gluing cabochons is to rough up the back of smooth cabochons with some sandpaper. (Black Onyx is a good example of a hard-to-glue smooth surface.) Peyote stitch will help secure large cabochons in place.

Adhesives by Sherry and Heidi

Two-part epoxy

You can get two-part epoxy at most hardware or craft stores (use transparent, if possible). Start by putting equal amounts of each part of the glue on scrap paper and mix together with a toothpick. You'll have about five minutes to use this glue before it sets. Try not to get the glue on your fingers as it's very sticky, and before you know it, your whole project will be sticky (it's very much like tree sap). Clean up with rubbing alcohol while the glue is still wet. Once it's dried, epoxy is hard to get out of Ultrasuede. Two-part epoxy dries in about 15 minutes. Always wash up with soap and water after use.

You can use two-part epoxy to glue all your jewelry findings to your finished beadwork, including pin backs and clip and post earring backs, and you can use it to glue end caps and bolo tips onto necklace cord. Use epoxy to glue cabochons to Ultrasuede or clear cabochons to foil. When gluing to foil, make sure to trim excess foil off before the glue sets too long — about 10 minutes at the most. This is also a great glue to use on concave items where you have a lot of space to fill up with glue.

Tacky glue

Aleene's Thick Designer "Tacky Glue" is user-friendly — your kids and pets can even use it. It comes in a wide top, so you can dip your toothpick directly into the container. Tacky glue cleans up with water, so if it gets on your Ultrasuede, a wet cotton swab cleans it right off. Remember, it's not intended for washable wearable.

Use a toothpick to spread tacky glue on the paper backing that will be glued to the back of your finished beadwork. Glue the Ultrasuede backing to the back of your piece using tacky glue as well.

Tacky glue is ideal for loomwork as well as gluing Ultrasuede to barrettes, brass necklace blanks, or bracelet cuffs. Apply the glue to the Ultrasuede rather than the brass.

Double-sided tape

Double-sided tape can be used on cabochons that will be captured with peyote stitch. This is a great alternative to glue because you can begin work immediately. It's effective on the back of smooth stones. Trace around the stone onto the tape with a permanent marker. Remove the stone and cut around the shape, ⅛ in. inside of the line you traced so the tape isn't flush up against the edges of the stone. You will find that if the tape is too close to the edge of the stone, your needle will get stuck in the tape when you're stitching. Find double-sided tape at firemountaingems.com, thermoweb.com, or your local craft store.

UFO glue

UFO glue stands for User Friendly Odorless. It's available in a thick and thin application. The bottle is easy to use, so you can apply the glue directly to the surface. UFO glue works great for small cabochons and metal. Apply the glue to the back of your sanded cabochon and carefully place the cabochon where you want it. Once pressure is applied, it sticks, so make sure your cabochon is lined up nicely before you apply any pressure. Hold for 50 seconds and then let the glue dry for 30 minutes before doing any beadwork. The glue needs to rest 24 hours for full adhesion. We don't recommend using UFO to glue clear cabochons to foil because it seems to like a rough surface best. You can find UFO glue at your local hardware store or theglueguy.com.

E-6000

Sherry uses E-6000 to attach cabochons or findings that will not be secured with a peyote stitch bezel. Always use E-6000 glue in a well-ventilated area and do not inhale the fumes. As with any glue, please read the warnings on the back of the label. If your cabochon is lightweight, UFO glue, epoxy, or double-sided tape are great alternatives.

Transparent cabochons should first be glued to foil. This shows the stone's true color rather than the foundation color. Once the stone has adhered to the foil, trim the excess with your scissors.

Be sure to read the labels! You'll learn what you need to know about safety precautions and how to most effectively use the product. Different adhesives work in different applications, so understanding the glue's properties before you begin will help you use it correctly. With time and practice, you'll find your favorite.

FINISHING

Finishing is so very important in beadwork. How you finish your piece can make or break its final appearance. Keep in mind that the backside of your beadwork should look as beautiful as the front. This means keeping your stitches neat and matching thread color to your desired backing.

Photo by Larry Sanders

Photo by Larry Sanders

Photo by Larry Sanders

Finishing by Heidi and Sherry

Putting the finishing touches on a piece is one of the most rewarding steps in the process. All your efforts come into place and you get to see how the piece is going to look and feel. This is the time to figure out if you want to add fringe, and what kind of clasp you want to use.

After your backing has been glued into place, you'll need to trim the excess Ultrasuede. Be careful here — you don't want to trim the foundation, only the Ultrasuede that extends past your foundation. This is where a nice pair of scissors comes in handy. Sometimes you need to cut into small tight curves, and sharp scissors with pointed tips work best for this.

Once the piece is all trimmed, you can start your edging. The edging holds the foundation and backing together. Heidi uses Simple Edging (Heidi's stitches, p. 23). With simple edging you can add one or two beads to make the loop bigger and give the edging a lacier look. Sherry uses Brick Stitch or Picot Stitch, which also gives the option of embellishment (Sherry's stitches, pp. 20 and 21).

No matter what you're making, the process is the same. Think of it as a S'more (we have all enjoyed those tasty treats at some point in our lives). The Ultrasuede is the graham cracker, and the chocolate and marshmallow are the lining and finding. But instead of eating it, you are going to seal the edges so the chocolate and marshmallow don't run out — in other words, you're sealing the Ultrasuede edges so the lining and finding glued in between aren't exposed.

For a post earring (**a** and **b**), punch a hole in the backing (the hole reamer is a great tool for this; see Tools, p. 16), push the post through the hole, and glue together (see Sherry's Paisley Earrings, p. 54). If you are making a French wire earring you'll want to check out Heidi's Trilobite Earrings (p. 84).

To finish a pin (**c** and **d**), cut out two holes with a utility knife on your backing where the pin back hinge and fastener rest. Push the pin back through those holes and glue (see Sherry's Free-form Brooch, p. 50, or Heidi's Tree Frog Pin, p. 88).

For a pendant without a bail, Heidi glues a long cylinder bead to the lining using tacky glue (**e** and **f**). This way you can string the pendant like a bead, giving it a nice clean look. Sherry uses a totally different technique in her pendant project (see Sherry's Art Pendant, p. 58). She tacks the cord to the back of the Lacy's Stiff Stuff with small stitches that will be hidden by a supporting base.

Finish a bracelet (**g** and **h**) as in Sherry's Half-inch Moon Cuff project (p. 62), or Heidi's Sterling Cuff Bracelet project (p. 80). Both are totally different techniques and totally rockin'.

Putting the clasp on a collar necklace can sometimes be tricky. One way Heidi adds a clasp is using the S'more technique (**i** and **j**). Sew the loop of the clasp onto the back of your foundation at the ends of your collar (this will add extra strength to the clasp); the loop will then be glued between the foundation and backing and hidden so only the clasp remains. When you edge the piece, work your beads around the clasp. Adding a clasp with an adjustable chain extension is always a great way to assure a good fit. Plus, sometimes you might want to wear your masterpiece over a turtleneck; the chain allows for flexibility. For other tips on finishing collars, see Sherry's Ammonite Collar project on p. 66, or Heidi's Ancient Spirals Collar on p. 92.

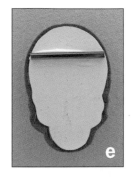

Photo by Larry Sanders

FRINGE

Sherry's Fringe

Photo by Larry Sanders

Photo by Larry Sanders

Photo by Larry Sanders

Fringe

Fringe can change the entire look of a design. Fringe is approached differently depending on the project. If your beadwork is busy, you may want to keep your fringe simple.

When stitching fringe onto a collar or pendant, begin at the center point at the bottom of your beadwork to help keep the sides even. When creating a free-form shape like a brooch, you can do free-form fringe. This also works with a cuff.

Photo by Larry Sanders

Simple fringe

I like simple fringe in a design when I don't want to overwhelm the piece, but enhance it. While this is quite similar in appearance to Heidi's fringe, the techniques are different. I always work off my brick-stitched edge beads.

Cut approximately 6 yd. (5.5m) of thread for a large project and 2–3 yd. (1.8-2.7m) for a smaller one, like an earring. Add a needle to each end of the thread. You will use half the thread for the right side of the beadwork, and half for the left side of the beadwork. Position an end bead (such as an 11º seed bead) at the center of the thread. String on your desired fringe from the bottom to top. (An example of simple fringe could be: 18 11º seed beads, a bugle bead, three crystals or Czech beads, and

an end bead.) Pass both needles through the entire strand of fringe and pass one needle through the center edge bead on your design. Now pass the other needle through the same bead. Pass one of the needles down through the edge bead on the right and the other needle through the edge bead on the left. You are now in position to do your fringe. Working both sides will ensure even fringe.

You now have a needle on both sides of the beadwork. Work the rest of your fringe up the sides of your collar or pendant. When finished, bury the thread somewhere in the beadwork, then knot and trim.

To create fringe with a V-shape or fan look, reduce the number of seed beads of each fringe as you travel up the sides of your design.

Photo by Larry Sanders

Free-form fringe

Free-form fringe looks great on a cuff or brooch, and you can start the thread anywhere in the piece. I love free-form the best because I get bored so easily! This is a fabulous way to use up beads left over from another project.

Thread a needle, make a tiny knot at one end, and trim the tail close to the end. Bury the thread somewhere in the beadwork to hide the knot and exit one of the brick stitch edge beads. Pick up the desired number of beads for the fringe. Add an end bead, sew back through all the fringe beads, and back into the edge bead. Or, make loops: Bring the needle up through a brick stitch edge bead, pick up seven to nine seed beads, and go back through the same edge bead. Continue alternating fringe with varying patterns and bead counts with loops along the edge beads. When finished, knot with several overhand knots, bury the thread in the beadwork, and trim the thread. Have a blast with this technique!

Fringe with drops

Single thread a needle, make a tiny knot, and trim the tail end close to the knot. Bury the thread somewhere in the beadwork, hiding the thread end, and exit one of the brick stitch edge beads. Pick up the desired fringe beads and decide how large you would like your loops to be around your drop bead. For example, I might string on eight 14ºs, a drop bead, and eight more 14ºs. Then, sew back up through the fringe beads and the edge bead. Continue around in this manner. When finished, knot, bury the thread in the beadwork, and trim the thread. If your drop beads are heavy, use doubled thread or reinforce by sewing through all the fringe strands a second time.

FRINGE

Heidi's Fringe

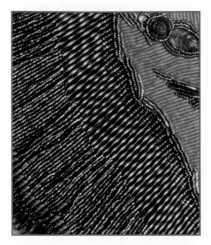

Fringe

Many designs can be stunning without fringe, and then there are those that just call for it. If you've edged your piece and it still isn't ready to hatch, by all means add some fringe. Everything looks good in fringe, and your masterpiece is born. Then again, if your piece looks great by itself, maybe you only need to add a simple drop. Sometimes the fringe can be distracting, take away from your piece, or make it too overwhelming.

When adding fringe, I like to work from the backside, and from the left to the right pushing the finished fringe to the left as I work. Working from the back positions the fringe behind the edging, not in front. If spaced properly, edging beads can help you space the fringe.

Basic tube-and-crystal fringe

This very easy technique creates wonderfully full and long fringe. Start with 1 yd. (.9m) of thread with a knot on one end and a #12 long needle on the other. At one end, push the needle between the foundation and backing to hide the knot, and come out through the back where you will add the fringe. String the following beads: four 9º beads, one tube bead, two 9º beads, two 4mm crystal beads, and five 15º beads. Sew back up through the crystal and the remaining beads in the strand. The five 15º beads will form a loop below the crystal and keep the thread from coming back up. Now sew through the front of your foundation, but behind the edging, and exit on the back side about 1/16–1/8 in. (2–3mm) down from where you started. Pull the fringe up next to your piece by laying it flat on your work surface. Hold the five 15º beads down on the surface with your left hand and pull the thread up using your right hand (this allows you to pull the strand of beads up to the edge of your piece, with the proper tension). You don't want to pull too hard or your beads will bunch up and not drape nicely. For your second round, string the following: six 9º beads, one tube bead, two 9º beads, three 4mm crystals, and five 15º beads. Repeat the process as in the first round. Each time you add a

new strand of beads, add two more 9º beads on the top and one extra crystal. By adding these extra beads, your strands will slowly get longer and fuller. When you get to the middle of your piece, simply count back so you will be subtracting the two 9º beads and one crystal, creating a mirror image to the side you just completed. I encourage you to use different beads and counts as you develop your own style.

Charming fringe

Charms add playfulness and fullness to a piece. They can also help you create a theme because they have different meanings. Start your fringe as you would for the basic tube-and-crystal fringe. The idea here is to use various bead sizes and textures to create fullness while changing the bead count to create depth. Once you're ready, add ten 9º beads, five 15º beads, one charm, and five more 15º beads. Go back up through the ten 9º beads and pull the strand up as described in the basic tube-and-crystal fringe. Start another round, this time adding ten 9º beads and maybe a stone cylinder bead. You get the idea — keep going, alternating the length and items you include.

Straight fringe

Straight fringe is so named because it's attached to a separate piece of Ultrasuede and glued on to the back of the piece so the fringe hangs straight down without disturbing the shape of the beadwork. For example, if the piece you are finishing has steep vertical sides and you add fringe all the way around it, the fringe will hang off to the sides rather than hang downward. Sometimes this can be spectacular; but it also can be time-consuming and heavy. First, determine where you want the fringe to start. Then measure straight across the back of your piece to the opposite side where the fringe will end. Cut your Ultrasuede 1-in. (2.5cm) wide and ½-in. (1.3cm) longer than your measurement. You can use a fine-tipped marker and space your fringe out on the Ultrasuede. This will help for needle placement.

Single-thread a #12 needle using 1 yd. of thread. Come up through one of the marked holes, and string the fringe. Use either of the two fringe techniques described above, but remember that the top portion of this fringe is going to be covered by the beadwork; you may want to use simple beads and patterns above the top as it will only be seen from behind. Hold the Ultrasuede and fringe up behind your beadwork where it will be attached to see how it looks and lays. Alter as needed. Once all the fringe is added, knot the thread and weave it into the fringe. Using tacky glue, spread the glue onto the backside of the fringed Ultrasuede, and adhere it into place on the back

of the beadwork. Once the glue has set, trim the excess Ultrasuede. For added security, sew the ends to the sides of the piece. You also can add straight fringe to a piece before you begin edging. Then, trim the straight fringe's Ultrasuede to the edge of the beadwork and add the edging for a nice clean finish. Heidi's Trilobite Earrings project (p. 84) gives you a great example of using this fringe.

This fringe can be used on other projects as well, such as lamp shades or bottles.

Because design concepts are so involved,
we've divided them into four categories:
Inspiration, Design, Color, and Texture.
We hope you can use all these concepts to
create your own masterpieces.

Design

INSPIRATION

Sherry

Photo by Larry Sanders

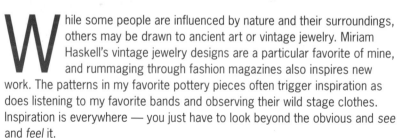

While some people are influenced by nature and their surroundings, others may be drawn to ancient art or vintage jewelry. Miriam Haskell's vintage jewelry designs are a particular favorite of mine, and rummaging through fashion magazines also inspires new work. The patterns in my favorite pottery pieces often trigger inspiration as does listening to my favorite bands and observing their wild stage clothes. Inspiration is everywhere — you just have to look beyond the obvious and *see* and *feel* it.

Your inspiration may lie in cabochons, buttons, or even a beautifully vibrant and colorful fabric! My neighbor is a fabulous pottery designer. The patterns he incorporates into his pieces inspire me all the time and have been responsible for many of my beaded designs. Dichroic glass is awesome for inspiring colors. There are so many hues within the glass stones that it's almost overwhelming! You can use a wide variety of bead colors to enhance these beauties. Look into the source and see what colors exist, or what shape it can become. I was never one to color inside the lines and I believe the grass doesn't always have to be green, nor the sky blue.

One of the things I find myself doing when exploring new ideas is looking beyond the actual object in front of me. What colors exist and how can I incorporate that into beads? There are so many amazing bead colors that it's easy to gather inspiration and match it to beads!

Heidi

Inspiration comes easily to me, as I get excited just looking at somebody else's junk. While I walk my dogs, I am always running into something that inspires me, whether it's moss growing on the forest floor with its green velvet touch, or the early morning frost.

I also look to animals for inspiration. When I'm walking, if I happen to cross paths with a deer or owl I take it as a sign; I go home and look up the animal's meaning. This animal may end up in one of my pieces or maybe the message will try to come through.

You can find inspiration in people as well. I first got the idea to do collar necklaces after seeing an article by Virginia Blakelock in the December 1988 *Threads* magazine. Virginia's work is so inspiring and amazing. I would never copy someone else's work, but if it wasn't for this article I might not have ventured into making large collar pieces.

Cabochons and vintage buttons found at garage sales or bead shows also can be inspirational. Emotions, such as happy or sad, can trigger an idea. Even a political, environmental, or spiritual feeling can lead to self-expression. Let the world know what you're feeling.

DESIGN

Sherry

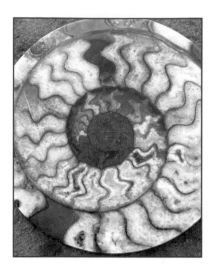

D esign is such a personal "animal." When I teach, I always urge my students to follow their hearts and just let a design happen. It isn't something that can be forced, it must flow from one's own soul. Finding your own creative niche can be an enriching and spiritual journey. Free-form embroidery's spontaneity allows me to change materials, stitches, or direction on a whim. The final product is never exactly known; the excitement is watching the beadwork develop its own personality.

I approach my artwork by thinking in shapes and colors. An odd-shaped cabochon may throw me into a designing frenzy. It helps sometimes to think of these individual pieces as puzzle pieces — just play with them until you have the perfect fit.

Architecture and shape within design are important to me, as I like to play with strength in a design, especially in my broad collars. Sometimes I embroider several pieces and play with their shapes to create a pleasing piece of wearable art. It's helpful to use an actual display bust to design a large piece. Like a dressmaker would, pin pieces of your embroidery to the form to see how your piece will look as it progresses.

When approaching a new piece of art, I often play with the cabochons and move them around — much like finding pieces to fit into a complex puzzle. The colors should complement each other, and the shapes should have a good visual fit.

The stones or buttons are almost always my focus when creating. Their shapes dictate the creation of the piece. If a stone is triangular, the design may take on that particular shape. The focal point is important in telling you where to place other beads and the shapes that will flow in your design.

I believe the key element to designing is playing. Look at the elements around you with a creative eye. That vintage button you've been hanging onto can be used instead of a cabochon, or you can use actual pieces of nature! I once used bamboo in a design that displayed a panda bear, and incorporated a refrigerator magnet into a beaded collar!

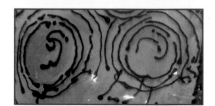

Heidi

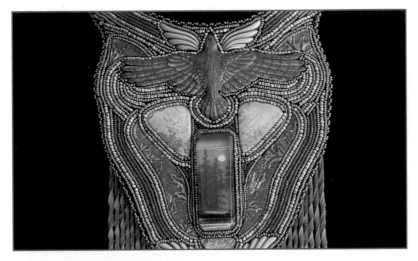

Once you have an idea or beautiful cabochon in mind, you need to transform it into a pattern. Basically this pattern is going to be the area that will be covered in beads.

You also need to think of what specific piece of jewelry you will be making. Here we will be talking about necklaces. If you are going to make a broad collar, it will take many hours, months, or maybe even years. You can make something elaborate but on a much smaller scale that won't take you as long to finish. In that case the focal point will be in a pendant or bib where the majority of beading is in the front, and you use a heavy cord or chain that wraps around your neck to finish, rather than beading the entire piece.

I have an assortment of necklace patterns I have made from old T-shirts or clothing patterns. The most important part of your pattern is the inside where it fits around your neck. You can cut up an old T-shirt, save the collar, and then cut the collar in the back and remove approximately 1 in. (2.5cm) to allow for the clasp. Make sure this fits your neck the way you want, and than trace it onto a sheet of paper. Make sure you leave enough room on the paper to lay out your idea or your cabochons.

Start by picking a center focal point: a stone, a button, even Grandma's old cameo. Lay the stone in the center of the paper pattern. Place other stones around to see what looks best to you. Move them around on the paper; try different locations and stones. There is no right or wrong way; it's all a matter of what looks good to you. If you're planning to incorporate an animal, get a photograph of the animal you wish to use and copy it to the desired size using a copier. (I copy mine on tracing paper so I can glue it to the Ultrasuede and actually stitch through it.) Cut out the animal and place it in various places, as you did the stones, until you find the spot where it wants to live (see more about this in my collar project on p. 92).

Even if you're not making an elaborate piece, it helps to lay your stones out on the paper so you can get an idea of where a chain or bail will need to be placed. My grandfather drew beautiful sketches of his carvings before he ever began carving; you might find it best to draw your design idea first. I have a little black book I keep new ideas in. However, I never design by drawing a piece first, because for me everything flows into place as I start working on it.

COLOR

Sherry

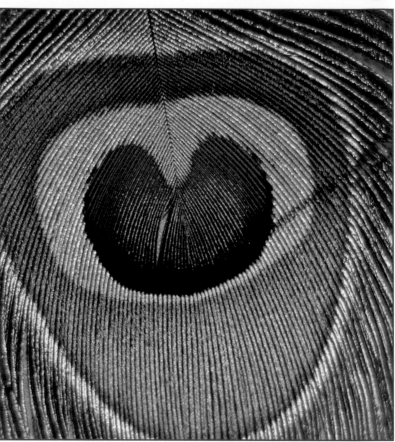

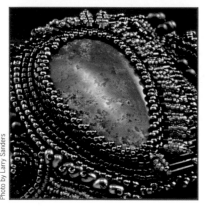

Photo by Larry Sanders

Photo by Larry Sanders

Once the stones are in place, the beadwork comes into play. Focusing on the stone, which literally becomes the "focal point" of the piece, I select the colors of the beads according to the colors of the stones. I like to work with a limited palette of seed beads, sometimes choosing only three basic colors. These basic colors can be a variety of different tones. For example, if I select purple, blue, and black I will vary my shades of each color. Being a former painter, I look at beads as small tubes of paint and use them to fill in my design by embroidering around the cabochons.

Seed beads come in such a vast variety of colors and finishes. Matte-finished beads stitched beside shiny ones allow the colors to pop. A color wheel is a good tool if you need help with color. Sometimes I place all of my tubes of beads on my table and lay them out beside each other to see what pleases my eye. Once again, this is a personal choice. One person's color choices will not necessarily be another's.

40   The Art of Bead Embroidery

Heidi

For me, color comes from nature. If you take a walk with nature, you can see that the Great Spirit has picked out all the colors for you. They all complement one another. Check out the moss growing on the rocks, or the bark on the trees. If you live in the city, take a nature walk to the library, where hundreds of books with pictures of nature are available. I'll bet if you look, you can find nature in cities. You even can get colors from rusty metal. Flowers are full of colors — not a bouquet of flowers but one individual flower. One flower has an enormous range of colors and they all work beautifully together.

Another fun way to find colors that work together is through a kaleidoscope. Not the kind that has the colors already in them — though those would work as well — but the kind that you can walk around with and point at anything (be careful here). My son Ben and I love to do this together. Try checking out your dog's face with a kaleidoscope. You will be amazed at how many different colors there are and how they complement one another.

When I am designing a necklace with a lot of cabochons, I only use different shades of metallic gold beads. The stones say it all; you don't want to distract from the beauty of the stone.

If I am embroidering a natural wonder such as an elk or hummingbird, I use colors that complement the animal and its surroundings. I believe it's best not to go overboard with color and that most times, less is more.

TEXTURE

Sherry

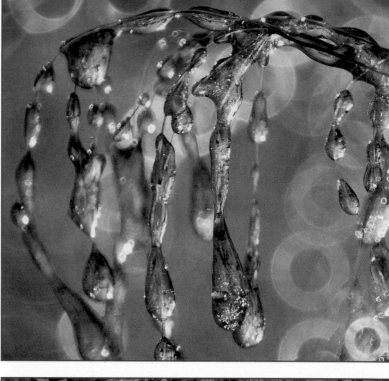

Photo by Larry Sanders

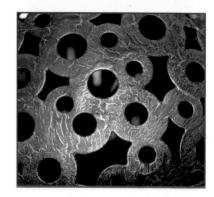

Texture is another element I like to experiment with. I feel this adds interest to the beaded piece. Create texture by using various sizes of beads while you embroider. Play with a round of 14ºs and switch to 11ºs, or throw a round of freshwater pearls into the design.

This is one reason the stop stitch is a personal favorite. Using a freshwater pearl or odd-shaped bead with a 14º seed bead as a stopper adds texture. Laying the same bead sideways adds a completely different look and brings a new texture to the beadwork.

Think of taking your beads on little road trips! Create paths that flow from one end of the design into the next, creating a "road map of beads."

Heidi

Texture is a wonderful thing to work into your designs. Just because something isn't flat on one side doesn't mean you can't incorporate it into your design. Be creative and string your beads around it to help hold it in place. Use different bead sizes to add depth. You don't always have to stitch the beads flat; make them stand up, so they pop out and say something. We all have an opinion, even our beads!

Are you ready to begin? Everything you've learned thus far comes together in the projects. So gather your supplies and tools and discover for yourself the art of bead embroidery.

Projects

Sherry

Let's begin with an easy project. It introduces backstitching. When I make a belt buckle, I like to use a rich, beautiful piece of Ultrasuede and allow it to show through the beadwork. In this project, the vintage button is enhanced by the suede and the simple beadwork surrounding the button. I've got some pretty cool guy friends who love belt buckles, including a couple of musicians! You can purchase belts with removable buckles at your local department store.

Materials:
- 25mm vintage button
- 1g 11º seed beads, gray matte metallic
- 2 10 x 8mm cabochons, riverstone
- 1g 14º seed beads, bronze
- 4 4mm freshwater pearls
- Belt buckle (Tandy Leather Company)

Tools:
- Beading needles, #12 or #13
- Toothpicks

Scissors
- Nymo B or D, color to match Ultrasuede

Stitches:
- Backstitch 2

Foundation:
- 4 x 4-in. (10 x 10cm) piece of Ultrasuede, complementary color to button

Adhesives:
- E-6000

VINTAGE BUTTON BELT BUCKLE

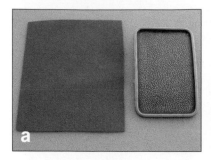

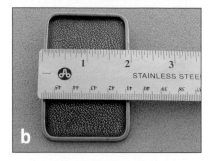

Preparing the suede

1. Start your project by selecting a buckle and suede to complement the button (**a**). Make sure the button fits within the parameters of the buckle.

2. Measure the buckle and cut the suede to the exact size of the buckle (**b**). Glue the button to the center of the suede with E-6000 and let dry for 20 minutes (**c**). (See adhesives, p. 26.)

Stitching

3. Single thread a needle with 2 yd. (1.8m) of beading thread and tie a knot at one end. Bring the needle up from the underside of the Ultrasuede (about a bead's width from the side of the button). Pull the thread until the knot is tight against the back of the Ultrasuede.

4. Design from the center out: Start the beadwork by backstitching a round of 11° gray beads around your cabochon (**d**).

5. Work backstitch 2 all the way around the button and weave the needle to the back of the suede. Pass the needle up from under the suede about a bead's-width away from the first round. If there is room, you can backstitch another round as shown (**e**).

6. Glue the two 10 x 8mm cabochons to the suede with E-6000, flush against the second round of backstitching. You may want to use a ruler to make sure the cabs are centered on the sides of the button (**f**).

7. Backstitch a round of the gray 11°s around the small cabochons (**g**).

8. Backstitch a single round of bronze 14°s around the cabs and the button (**h**).

9. Add freshwater pearls (treating them as you would a bugle bead, p. 20), stitching lengthwise to the inner corners of the cab and the button (**i**).

Finishing

10. This is the easiest finishing ever done! Roll a thin layer of E-6000 on the back of the beadwork (**j**) and press the beadwork into the belt buckle. Let dry. Wear your buckle with your favorite pair of jeans!

Keep your stitches firm and snug, but don't pull too tightly or the suede will buckle and the work will shrink.

Sherry

I enjoy creating brooches and I view them as miniature works of art. I do a lot of large–bead projects, so these small designs are a fabulous break because I can create one during the day and be ready to wear it in the evening! This is a free-form project, so you should experiment with bead shapes and colors to create an original work of art, based on the instructions I've provided.

Materials:
- 16 or 18mm cabochon, (16mm flower by Earthenwood Studio)
- Less than 1g each $14^{\underline{o}}$ and $11^{\underline{o}}$ seed beads in two or three colors
- Various embellishment beads, such as bugle beads or any kind of bead that appeals to you!

Tools:
- Toothpick
- Scissors
- Various needles sized to accommodate bead holes
- Nymo B or D, color to match Ultrasuede
- Fine–point permanent black marker

Stitches:
- Peyote, Backstitch 2, Stop stitch, Picot brick stitch

Foundation and backing:
- 2 x 2-in. (5 x 5cm) piece of Lacy's Stiff Stuff (my piece is dyed gray)
- 2 x 2-in. piece of Ultrasuede in color to match your beads

Adhesives:
- Double–sided tape
- UFO glue

FREE-FORM BROOCH

Preparing the cabochon and foundation

1. Use double-sided tape to adhere your cabochon to the Lacy's Stiff Stuff (**a**). (See adhesives, p. 26.)

2. This is a free-form beading project. However, if you are not comfortable with this method, feel free to draw an outline around the perimeters of the cabochon to use as a guide. You can also draw a pleasing design for the rest of the pin.

Stitching

3. Single thread a needle with 2 yd. (1.8m) of beading thread and tie a knot at one end. Bring the threaded needle up from under the Lacy's Stiff Stuff (about a bead's width from the side of the cabochon). Pull the thread until the knot is tight against the back.

4. Begin backstitching a round of 14º beads around your cabochon (see p. 19). String on two 14º seed beads, lay them against the cabochon, pass the needle back through the backing, and snug the new beads up against the last bead stitched. Work backstitch 2 all the way around the cabochon, ending with an even number of beads (**b**). Note: If you are uncomfortable with the tiny 14ºs, please feel free to use 11ºs.

5. You are now ready to begin capturing the cab with peyote stitch (see p. 19). Working from the round you just backstitched, bring the needle straight up from beneath the backing and position it between two beads in the round. Pass the needle through one 14º seed bead. String one 14º seed bead on the needle, skip the next bead in the backstitched round, and sew through the next bead (**c**). Continue around the cabochon to create a beaded bezel.

6. After you've peyote stitched around the cabochon, bury the thread in the

Make needle threading easier by wetting the end of the thread, cutting the thread at an angle, and pushing the needle onto the thread.

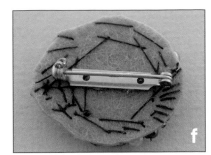

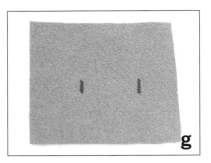

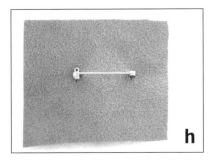

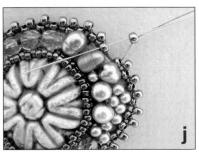

beadwork by passing the needle between the cab and the seed beads, exiting on the back side of the beadwork. You are now in position to start bead embroidery with backstitch.

7. Work one bead at a time when working with the larger beads, pearls, and crystals. Always go through the larger beads twice, using the stop stitch technique (see p. 20) to secure them. Follow the shape of the cabochon, using seed beads, bugle beads, pearls, or any other found object that pleases you (**d**). My ultimate goal is to persuade you to experiment with texture and design.

8. Once you've completed the bead embroidery around the cab, bring the needle to the back of the beadwork, make a few tiny stitches to secure the thread, and trim.

Finishing

9. Attach the pin back: When your brooch is beaded to your satisfaction, carefully cut out the design as close to the beadwork as you can without cutting the threads (**e**). Use a toothpick to roll a thin layer of UFO glue onto the pin back, and adhere it to the center of the back of the beadwork (**f**). Let dry.

10. Place the Ultrasuede on top of the pin and mark the location of both of the pin ends with a marker (**g**). Cut a small slit at both marks, open the pin back, and insert it through the slits in the Ultrasuede so the bar is hidden and the marks are on the inside. Use the toothpick to roll a thin layer of UFO glue to the inside of your piece (between the beadwork and the suede). Smooth the backing and let dry (**h**).

11. Edging: You will now finish the edges using picot brick stitch (see p. 21). Trim the suede to the same shape as your beadwork. To edge the brooch, thread a needle with a comfortable length of single thread (12 in./30cm is usually good). Tie a knot at the end and bring the needle near the edge of your beadwork, burying the knot in the beadwork so it is hidden from view. The thread is now anchored. With the needle exiting the edge of the brooch, work picot brick stitch around the beadwork to finish the edges (**i**). When you have reached the starting point, go down through the first bead and bury the thread in the beadwork (**j**). Tie several small knots, and trim the threads. You've now completed the edging, and you're ready to wear your dazzling brooch.

Sherry

Don't let the fact that these are earrings limit your thinking! These cool shapes can be created and used as patches for jeans or sewn onto your favorite hat. Because these are small creations, they're a great way to use up the "bead soup" that gathers after a larger project. I always have a small pile of leftover beads that I place in a zip-top bag and save for earring designs.

Materials:
- 2 15 x 7mm teardrop-shaped stones
- 1g 14º seed beads in three colors
- 10–12 6º seed beads
- 2 4–8mm donut-shaped beads
- 4–6 4mm crystals or glass beads
- 10–12 2–3mm freshwater pearls
- 15–20 size 2 bugle beads
- 2 post earring backs with ear nuts
- White scrap paper for designing

Tools:
- Toothpicks or dowel
- Scissors
- Various needles sized to accommodate bead holes

- Nymo B, color to match Ultrasuede

Stitches:
- Backstitch 2, Stop stitch, Picot brick stitch

Foundation and backing:
- 2 2 x 2-in. (5 x 5cm) pieces of Lacy's Stiff Stuff
- 2 2 x 2-in. pieces of Ultrasuede in color to match your beads

Adhesives:
- E-6000
- Two-part epoxy
- Tacky glue

PAISLEY EARRINGS

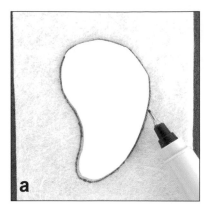

a

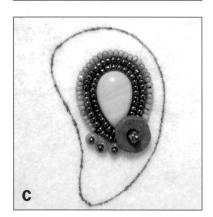

b

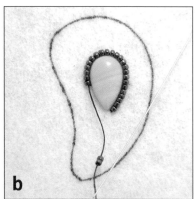

c

d

Preparing the cabs and backing

1. To begin this project, draw a desired shape on scrap paper. I used a paisley shape, but feel free to experiment with any shape. When you are satisfied with your design, cut out the shape to create a paper template. Trace the design onto a 2 x 2-in. (5x5cm) piece of Lacy's Stiff Stuff. Flip the template over and trace it again on a second piece of Lacy's Stiff Stuff (**a**) to create a mirror image for the second earring.

2. Using a small amount of E-6000, adhere each cabochon separately to the Lacy's Stiff Stuff. Make sure the stones are centered in the traced pattern. Let dry for 20 minutes.

Stitching

3. Single thread a needle with 2 yd. (1.8m) of beading thread and tie a knot at one end.

4. Bring the needle up through the Lacy's Stiff Stuff from the back side about a bead's width away from the stone. Pick up two 14º beads and begin working backstitch 2 (see p. 19) around the cabochon (**b**).

5. Once the first round is completed, backstitch a second round of 14º beads around the outside of the first round.

6. Now that you've made a base of beads around the cabochons, you can start stitching embellishment beads (**c**). Following your earring's shape, continue adding rounds of seed beads and embellish with crystals, bugles, and pearls. Keep your tension tight, but not so tight that the Lacy's begins to pull and pucker. When the beading is complete, tie off the thread on the back of the beadwork by tying a few overhand knots. Trim the threads.

7. Cut around the beadwork, leaving an approximately ¹⁄₁₆-in. (2mm) border all the way around for finishing (**d**).

8. If you have not been stitching both earrings simultaneously, bead your other earring to match the first.

9. Lay both earrings flat on your work surface, with the front side down, and glue the earring finding to the backing (**e**). Let dry for 20 minutes.

10. Pierce a small hole in the center of a piece of Ultrasuede that is slightly larger than your earring. Slide the Ultrasuede over the top of the earring back, apply a thin layer of tacky glue with a toothpick between the backing and Ultra-suede, and press together (**f**). Clean up any glue that may seep out around the edges. Let dry for 20 minutes.

11. When your pieces are dry, trim the excess Ultrasuede from the edges of the earring (**g**).

12. To begin edging, thread a needle with a ½ yd. (46cm) of thread and tie a knot at one end. Bring the needle down through the edge of the beadwork (between the pearls is a good place) and exit between the Lacy's Stiff Stuff and the Ultrasuede.

When working on earrings, it's sometimes helpful to bead both at the same time to ensure that you are doing both exactly the same.

13. Pick up three 14º seed beads. Measure about one seed bead over from the thread and sew down through the edge of the beadwork and the Ultrasuede. Bring your needle back up through the third seed bead and pull gently (**h**).

14. Pick up two seed beads. Measure one seed bead over and sew down through both layers again. Sew back up through the second seed bead. Repeat around the beadwork's edge.

15. Once you've completed the edging and are back where you started, string one seed bead, and sew through the first edge bead. Weave the needle into the beadwork, tie several knots, and trim the thread.

16. Repeat steps 12–15 to finish the second earring.

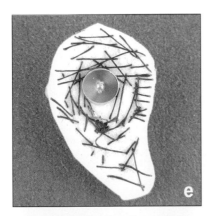

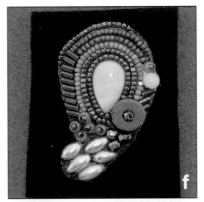

Sherry

Pendants are a lot of fun! You can make the cord as long or as short as you'd like, depending on your style. For this project, experiment with beads that are similar in size, so you won't be using a large stone as the focal point. This will allow you to play with "beaded paths" in a design. Pendants can be big or small, depending on your personal preference. I, for one, have never been quiet about what I wear. My thoughts? The bigger, the bolder, the better!

Materials:

Pendant:
- 1g each 14º seed beads in three colors
- 5g 11º seed beads
- 1g size 3 bugle beads
- 4–8 freshwater pearls and any other desired embellishment beads
- Fringe beads:
  11 gold charms or drops
  11 6mm round beads or pearls
  11 4mm crystals or fire-polished beads
- Scrap paper

Cord:
- 24 4mm pearls
- 12 6mm freshwater pearls
- 20g 11º seed beads
- 24 4mm crystals or fire-polished beads
- Flexible beading wire, .019
- 2 crimp beads
- Clasp

Tools:
- Various needles sized to accommodate bead holes
- Toothpick
- Scissors
- Nymo B, black
- Fine-point permanent marker

Stitches:
- Peyote, Backstitch 2, Stop stitch, Brick stitch

Foundation, lining, and backing:
- 5 x 5-in. (12.7 x 12.7cm) piece of Lacy's Stiff Stuff
- Poster board
- 5 x 5-in. piece of Ultrasuede in color to match your beads

Fringe:
- Fringe with drops

Adhesives:
- Tacky glue

ART PENDANT

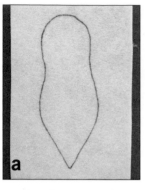

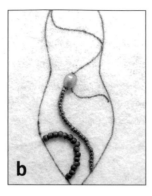

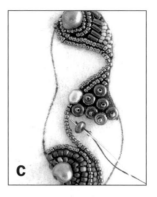

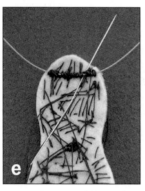

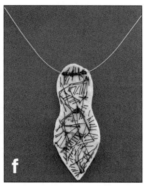

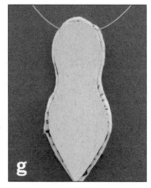

Planning the design

1. Create your pendant shape by drawing some designs on scrap paper until you have one you'd like to use.

2. Cut out the template and trace the design onto the Lacy's Stiff Stuff (**a**). Draw lines on your design to create paths, and designate where the beads will fill in the spaces. Keep in mind that you can change directions any time you like, as the lines will be covered with beads as you begin stitching!

Stitching the pendant

3. Single thread a needle with 2 yd. (1.8m) of beading thread and knot one end. Bring the needle up from the back side of the Lacy's Stiff Stuff. Following the lines you just drew, begin backstitching with seed beads. Then make beaded paths with bugle beads and seed beads. To keep the curves gentle, you may need to stitch only one bead at a time in some places (**b** and **c**). Using seed beads and embellishment beads, completely backstitch the entire piece using stop stitches and backstitch 2 (see pp. 19–20).

Trimming and finishing

4. When you're pleased with the design, carefully cut the foundation around the beadwork, leaving a 1/16-in. (2mm) edge (**d**). Be careful not to cut any threads.

5. Turn the beadwork over. Lay a 32-in. (81.2cm) piece of flexible beading wire down on the back of your beadwork, in a half-circle shape that crosses the top edges of the pendant. Try to envision where you want the necklace strands to lay on your neck.

6. Single thread a needle with beading thread and knot one end. Hold the beading wire in place and whip stitch (make a series of overhand stitches) it to the Lacy's until the wire is secured to the backing. Hold the beading wire in place while stitching around the piece. You are essentially "tacking" down the flexible beading wire (**e** and **f**).

7. When you've reached the end, tie a knot on the back of the beadwork, and trim.

8. Lay the beadwork on a piece of poster board and trace around it. Cut the poster board so it is approximately 1/8 in. (3mm) smaller than the pendant. Adhere the poster board to the beadwork (**g**) with tacky glue. Let dry for 20 minutes.

9. Glue a piece of Ultrasuede to the beadwork and poster board (**h**). Let dry.

10. Carefully cut around the beadwork and the Ultrasuede (**i**). You are now in position to begin edging your pendant. Single thread a needle with beading thread and tie a knot

at one end. Bury the knot in the beadwork. Measure about one seed bead over from the thread and sew down through the Lacy's Stiff Stuff and the Ultrasuede. Work brick stitch edging all the way around the pendant (**j**) (see p. 20).

11. When you reach the starting point again, pick up one bead and sew through the first bead. Weave your thread through the beadwork, and tie several knots, making sure all the knots are hidden. Trim the threads.

Stringing the necklace

12. Lay the pendant and the beads for the neck strap in front of you. Decide what pattern you would like, and string until the necklace is as long as you'd like it (**k**).

13. When you've reached the end of the strand, string on a crimp bead, four 11ºs, one clasp half, and four more 11ºs. Pass the beading wire back through the crimp bead. Pull snug so no gaps are showing between beads. Flatten the crimp bead to secure the beading wire. Repeat on the other side of the necklace (**l, m, n**).

Adding fringe

14. Now add the fringe to further enhance your design. Cut approximately 6 yd. (5.5m) of thread. Add a needle to each end of the thread. You'll use half the thread for the right side of the pendant, and half for the left side of the pendant.

15. Hold both needles so you have 3 yd. (2.7m) of thread on each side in front of you. Using the fringe with drops technique (p. 31), string the beads for your center fringe arrangement, ending with a charm. My center fringe is 1¾-in. (4.4cm) long, and I strung six 11ºs, a bugle, an 11º, a 4mm pearl, an 11º, a 4mm crystal, an 11º, six 14ºs, and a charm. Pick up six 14ºs, and sew back through the fringe beads so both needles are exiting the top bead. Bring both needles through the center edge bead on the pendant (**o**).

16. Working with one needle, sew through the edge bead on the right of the center bead, and sew through the edge bead on the left of the center bead with the other needle. You are now in position to work the rest of the fringe. Continue working each needle from the center out, adding fringe to the edge beads along the bottom of the pendant. So my fringe would form a V-shape to follow the pendant's shape, I gradually decreased the number of seed beads at the top of the fringe as I worked up both sides of the pendant. I picked up five beads for the second strand, four for the third, and three for the last two (**p**).

17. Once you've finished the fringe, weave the thread through the beadwork, tie a few knots, hide them in the beads, and trim the threads. Your necklace is now ready to wear.

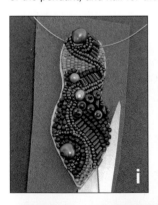

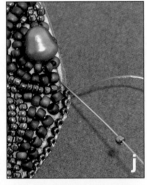

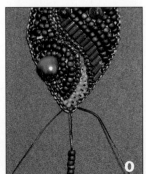

Sherry

I love bold statements when it comes to beaded adornments. That's what drives me to create these highly embellished arm ornaments. The possibilities seem endless when deciding where to place a certain pearl or round of bugles. I love the little moon face that was designed by Earthenwood Studios and just had to use it on a cuff. Choose what you love as a focal point ... follow your heart, and you'll never go wrong.

Materials:
- Brass cuff blank, ½ in. (1.3cm) wide
- Cabochon to fit ½-in. cuff (I used a cool face cabochon by Earthenwood Studios)
- 5g each 14° seed beads in two or three colors
- 10g 11° seed beads for edging
- 5g bugle beads
- Assorted 3mm, 4mm, and 6mm freshwater pearls
- 3g 8° seed beads

Tools:
- Toothpick
- Scissors

- Various needles sized to accommodate bead holes
- Nymo B, black
- Fine-point permanent marker

Stitches:
- Peyote, Backstitch 2, Stop stitch, Brick stitch

Foundation and backing:
- 1 x 7-in. (2.5 x 17.7cm) piece of Lacy's Stiff Stuff
- 1 x 7 in. piece of Ultrasuede in color to match your beads

Adhesives:
- E-6000
- Tacky glue

HALF-INCH MOON CUFF

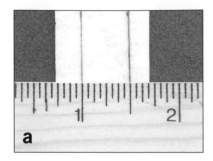

a

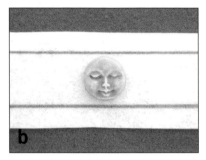

b

c

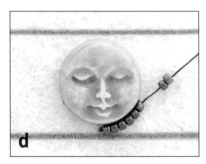

d

e

Preparing the cuff and cabochon

1. Begin this project by measuring the length and width of the brass cuff. Then draw the size of the cuff onto the Lacy's, leaving an extra ¼-in. (6mm) of Lacy's all the way around (**a**). This will *not* be beaded on and will be cut off later.

2. Play with the arrangements of your stones. Keep in mind that you will be backstitching around the stones, so allow for a bead space around the stones when gluing close to the edges of the ½-in. (1.3cm) template. When you're happy with an arrangement, move to the next step.

3. Use E-6000 to glue the cabochon into place on the Lacy's and set aside to dry (see adhesives, p. 26). Wipe off any excess glue that seeps out around the cab (**b**). Dry for 15 minutes.

4. While waiting for your cabochon to dry, get your cuff ready. Using the toothpick, roll a thin layer of tacky glue on the underside of the brass cuff (the part that will be against your skin). Carefully adhere the suede to the cuff, leaving excess Ultrasuede on the edges. Smooth the Ultrasuede against the cuff with your fingers to ensure there are no air pockets between the cuff and the Ultrasuede. Let it dry, then trim the suede to approximately ¹⁄₁₆ in. (2mm) larger than the blank. Do not cut the suede flush against the brass cuff. You will need an edge for finishing in the final steps (**c**).

Stitching

I like to use 14ºs around the cabochons because they don't overpower the cabochon on a smaller cuff. I also like to start beading around the cabochon first to give myself a starting point for the design. The cabochon is the focal point and is enhanced by the beads.

5. You are now ready to begin backstitching around the cabochon (see p. 19). Single thread a needle and tie a knot at one end. (Use single thread because you will make several passes through the beads.) Bring the needle up from the back side of the Lacy's about a bead's width from the side of the cabochon. Pull the thread until the knot is tight against the Lacy's.

6. String on two 14º seed beads, lay them snugly against the cabochon, and go back through the Lacy's next to the last bead picked up. Then sew from the back to the front, exiting the Lacy's on the left of the first bead strung. Sew through the beads one more time and exit the second bead (**d**).

7. Pick up two more beads, go down through the Lacy's next to the fourth bead, and come back up between the first and second beads. Sew through the second, third, and fourth beads again, and pick up two more beads. Repeat until you have encircled the entire cabochon (**e**).

Embroidering with backstitch and stop stitches

8. Begin embroidering the rest of the cuff with backstitch 2 and stop stitch (see pp. 19–20). When stitching a large bead, always make sure to stitch through it twice. Fill in around the larger beads with smaller beads, such as tiny 14ºs (**f**). Think of this as painting with beads.

Note: As you work, check the beadwork by laying it against the cuff to see how it fits. If your stitches are tight, they can pull the Lacy's, making it smaller. If you find you are doing this, ease up a little on tension. You always can add more beads to the design around the parameters of the piece so it fits properly.

9. After you've embroidered the entire cuff and are satisfied with the results, make sure the beads are secure and the stitches aren't loose (**g**).

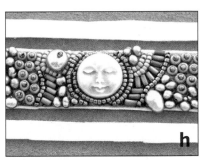

Finishing

10. After you complete the embroidery, lay the beaded piece against the cuff to see how it fits. If you find that you pulled too tightly on your stitches, you may have to add a couple more rounds of beads at the ends. Carefully trim the ¼-in. allowance on both sides of the beadwork as close to the beadwork as you can without cutting the threads (**h**).

11. Using a toothpick, roll a thin layer of tacky glue onto the backside of the beaded piece and glue to the top of the cuff (**i**). Let it dry about 20 minutes.

12. To edge the cuff, use brick stitch (see p. 20). Thread a needle with a 1-yd. (.9m) single strand of Nymo and knot one end. Sew into the beadwork at the edge to anchor the thread. With the needle exiting the top edge of the cuff, pick up an 11º bead and sew up through the Lacy's and the suede. Before tightening the stitch, sew down through the bead. The bead will stand out from the edge of the piece. Pick up another 11º and continue around the entire edge of the cuff, sewing through the Lacy's and the Ultrasuede to surround the brass cuff (**j**). The idea is to connect the two pieces together.

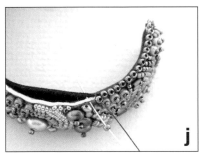

13. When you've edged around the cuff and your last bead meets the first bead, go down through the first bead to join them. Bring the needle through a few beads on the beadwork, making several small knots and hiding them in the beads. Trim the thread as close to the beadwork as you can without cutting into your beadwork. You're done! Wasn't that fun?

Sherry

Beaded collars are by far my favorite creations. They can be classy and elegant or rock-and-roll inspired. The design possibilities are virtually unlimited. The inspiration for this collar came from the cool ammonite used as the focal point. Cabochons provide me with tons of inspiration because of their endless shapes and colors. For me, a huge part of the fun in coming up with a new design is the hunt for the perfect focal point. I encourage you to play with design as much as you can, as it can be just as much fun as the actual beading.

Materials:
- Ammonite cabochon or button that appeals to you. (My ammonite is from Gary Wilson, and the free-form turquoise is from S&S Lapidary.)
- 30g 14º three-cut Charlottes
- 50g 11º seed beads that enhance your button or stone
- 5g 8º seed beads
- 144 6mm Czech beads
- 30g 5mm bugle beads
- Clasp (Beyond Beadery)
- 3 16-in. strands 4 — 8 mm freshwater pearls
- Various beads for embellishment

Tools:
- Dowel
- Scissors

- Various needles sized to accommodate bead holes
- Nymo B, black

Stitches:
- Peyote, Backstitch 2, Stop stitch, Brick stitch

Foundation and backing:
- Lacy's Stiff Stuff, dyed to match your beads (if desired)
- Ultrasuede in color to match your beads

Adhesives:
- E-6000
- Tacky glue

AMMONITE COLLAR

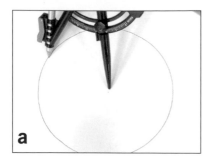

a

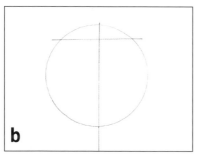

b

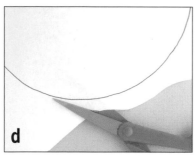

c

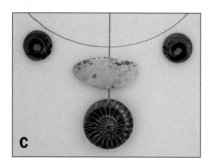

d

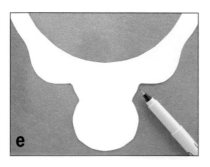

e

Planning the design

1. For a 15-in. (38cm) necklace, draw a 5½-in. (14cm) diameter circle with a compass (**a**) on a sheet of paper (adjust size for a smaller or larger collar). This is the inner edge of the collar. Draw a vertical line through the center. Extend the line a few inches below the circle to delineate the center front.

2. Measure 1 in. (2.5cm) down from the top of the circle on the centerline and make a mark. Draw a horizontal line through the circle at this mark (**b**). This line defines the neckpiece's back edges to achieve a curved fit. This size fits most necklines, but most certainly can be adjusted. Keep in mind that you will be adding your clasp in the final stages and this will add about 2 in. (5cm) to your paper template. I often place this paper template around my own neck after cutting to see how it fits. If I find I would like the neckpiece larger or smaller, I adjust the initial circumference using the compass.

3. Play with design by placing the stones on the paper in various arrangements. Find a design that makes you happy and trace around the stones on the paper to remember your placement (**c**). This sheet of paper is your template, which will guide you in designing the collar.

4. Using your center mark as a guideline, draw the basic shape. Measure 1–1½ in. (2.5–3.8cm) from the center point (this will vary based on cabochon size), tapering to approximately ¼-in. (6mm) width in the back to accommodate the clasp. At this point, fold the paper in half on the centerline. This assures that you are perfectly even on both sides of your template. Cut out this template (**d**) and trace it on a sheet of Lacy's Stiff Stuff with permanent marker (**e**). Do *not* cut out the Lacy's yet. You will trim away the extra after completing the bead embroidery.

Gluing and stitching

5. Glue the cabochons onto the Lacy's with E-6000 and let dry for at least 20 minutes. While the stones are drying, take some time to think about what you would like to do with your design. You can draw a design with a permanent marker to plan your work. Some folks prefer to let the beads guide them, and others are planners. There is no rule in this instance!

6. Backstitch a base round of 11º seed beads around each cabochon. The cabochons become the focal point. I like to backstitch a few rounds around the cabochons before venturing into the bead embroidery (**f**).

7. Begin embroidering the rest of the collar with beaded backstitch 2 (**g**). Keep the stitches snug, but don't pull the Lacy's because it may pucker. Always make sure you stitch through a large bead twice to ensure that it will be secure and not bobble around on your foundation. If you are using an especially large or rounded bead, dab a small dot of glue to the back of the bead to hold it securely in place. Follow the shape of the cabochon and use seed beads, bugle beads, "fun beads," and freshwater pearls. Think of this project as a collage. I like to create paths with the beads. My goal is for you to experiment with texture as you backstitch. If you're not one to just go with the flow, draw your design directly onto the Lacy's with a permanent marker. This is your time to have fun, listen to your inner voice, follow your heart, and bead.

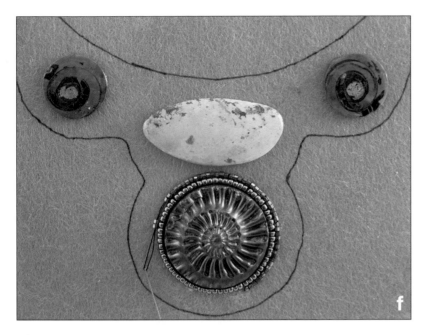

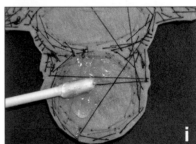

8. When you have about 6 in. (15cm) of thread left, tie a knot on the backside of the beadwork and trim the thread. Begin again by knotting a new thread, sewing up from the back of the beadwork, and continuing.

9. After you have embroidered your entire collar and are satisfied with the results, make sure your beads are secure and your stitches are tight.

Trimming and finishing

10. When you've completed your beadwork, knot the thread on the back and trim. Carefully (*very carefully!*) cut around your design, allowing approximately a 1/16 – 1/8 in. (2–3mm) of an edge for finishing (**h**).

11. Using a dowel, roll a thin, even layer of tacky glue across the entire back surface of the neckpiece (**i**). There is no right or wrong side to the Ultrasuede; one side is smoother and one is rougher. It is a matter of preference. Place the glued side down on the Ultrasuede and smooth it so there are no bumps or air pockets. Let dry for at least 20 minutes. Trim the Ultrasuede to the same shape as the beadwork (**j**).

12. Use brick stitch (see p. 20) to edge the neckpiece. Thread a needle with a 1-yd. (.9m) length of single strand Nymo and knot one end. Sew into the beadwork at the edge to anchor the thread, hiding the knot on the back of the beadwork. With the needle exiting the top edge of the beadwork, pick up an 11º and sew up through both the foundation and the suede. Before tightening the stitch, sew down through the bead so it stands out from the edge. Pick up another 11º and continue around the entire piece, sewing through the edge of the foundation and the edge of the Ultrasuede (**k**). When you've edged around the neckpiece and the last bead meets the first, go down through the first bead to attach the two. Sew through a few beads on the collar, making several small knots in the beadwork while hiding them in the beads. Trim the thread as close to the beadwork as you can, taking care not to cut your work.

AMMONITE COLLAR

Before cutting out the beadwork, check to make sure all the beads are secure. If you used larger pearls or odd-shaped beads, they can be tacked down with a small dab of glue applied to the back of the bead with a toothpick.

k

13. One of the reasons I use 11º beads for the edging is so I can run my threads through the holes several times. You will be doing this with the clasp. Double thread a needle and knot the ends together. Bring the needle down through the beadwork, hiding it carefully at the edge of the neckpiece. Sew up through one of the edge beads at the back of the neckpiece where the clasp will be attached. String on two 11ºs, a 6mm embellishment bead, three 11ºs, half the clasp, and three 11ºs. Go back through the 6mm, pick up two more 11ºs, and go through the next edge bead (**l** and **m**). Repeat the thread path as many times as needed for strength.

14. Repeat step 13 on the other side of the collar to connect the other clasp half.

Adding fringe

15. Now the embroidery work is done. It's time to decide if you would like to add fringe to your collar. Another reason I like to use 11º beads on my edges is because they can accommodate more thread passes for fringe techniques. Decide what type of fringe you would like to use in your design (see p. 30). I've kept my fringe simple in this project and selected straight fringe. Fringe can enhance your design or become the dominant design element. I felt my cabochons were very strong and required nothing more than a simple accent fringe.

l

m

16. Cut approximately 6 yd. (5.5m) of thread. Add a needle to each end of the thread. You will use half the thread for the right side of the collar, and half for the left side of the collar.

17. Hold both needles up so you have 3 yd. (2.7m) on each side in front of you. String the beads for your center fringe pattern, passing both needles up through the beads so they are exiting the top bead. With one needle, sew through the center edge bead on your design. Now sew the other needle through the same bead.

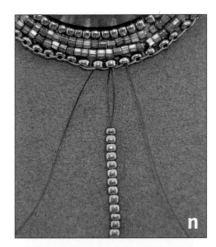

n

18. Working with one needle, sew through the edge bead on the right of the center bead, and sew the other needle through the edge bead on the left of the center bead (**n** and **o**). You are now in position to work the rest of the fringe (working both sides ensures even fringe). Continue working each needle from the center out, adding fringe to the edge beads along the bottom of the collar. For my fringe, I started my first strand with 13 11°s, a 5mm bugle, an 11°, a 6mm Czech bead, an 11°, a 6mm Czech bead, an 11°, a 6mm Czech bead, an 11°, and a 14° stop bead. I reduced each strand by one bead as I worked up the collar sides (**p**). When I reached eight 11°s on the fringe strand, I kept that number for the remainder of the fringe to keep it hanging nicely.

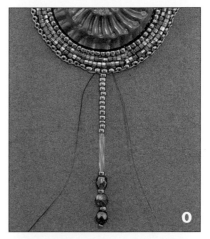

o

19. When you find you have about 6 in. (15cm) of thread remaining, weave into the beadwork and tie several knots, hiding them in the beadwork. Begin a new thread where you left off.

20. If you have selected a heavy fringe, sew back through the beads again.

21. When you've finished the fringe, weave the excess thread through the embroidered beadwork tying knots and hiding them in the beads. Trim the threads. You're finished! Try on your fabulous collar!

p

Heidi

This is a basic embroidery project. You may design your box so the bead embroidery goes around the outside rather than the top, if you like. The polymer clay ammonite works well with the stone box, but try other boxes you might find at your local craft store, such as wood or cardboard, or keep your eye out for something at a yard sale to re-invent. You can bead around cabochons, buttons, or whatever your box seems to require.

Materials:
- Box with flat lid (Fire Mountain Gems)
- Cabochon or focal point (Ammonite from Loco Lobo)
- 10g 15º seed beads, metallic gold

Tools:
- #12 sharp needle
- Nymo B
- Toothpicks

- Cotton swabs
- Scissors

Stitches:
- Backstitch 8, Webbing

Foundation:
- Ultrasuede

Adhesives:
- Two-part epoxy
- Tacky glue

AMMONITE BOX

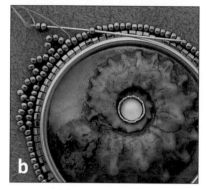

Designing the beadwork

1. Your design depends on your box. Does it have a round lid or is it square? This ammonite is the perfect size for this stone box. Choose a focal stone that complements your box.

2. Select Ultrasuede that complements the color of the box and the cabochon.

3. The bead color you choose should reflect the box and cabochon colors. The ammonite is beautiful by itself, so my choice is to use only 15º metallic gold seed beads for this piece.

Gluing and stitching

4. Glue the cabochon to the Ultrasuede using two-part epoxy: Spread the glue on the back of your cabochon with a toothpick, firmly press the cabochon into place, and use a cotton swab and rubbing alcohol to clean up any excess glue. Allow the glue to set for at least 15 minutes before stitching any beads.

5. Single thread a #12 sharp needle with 1 yd. (.9m) of beading thread and tie a knot at one end. Push the needle up through the Ultrasuede, next to the cabochon. Pick up eight 15º beads and work backstitch 8 (see p. 22) all the way around the cabochon, then sew through the round of beads again to bring the beads snug against the stone and strengthen the round.

6. Add a second round of beads using the same technique as in step 5 (**a**).

7. After you have finished the second round, begin the webbing (see p. 22). Start by exiting a bead on the last round, and picking up five 15º beads. Skip

three beads and sew into the fourth. Continue working webbing around the whole cabochon (**b**).

8. Next you will tack the webbing down to the foundation. Using your needle, pull the third (or middle) bead of the first five-bead webbing and position it so it forms a point as shown (**c**). Tack it in place to give it a nice centered look. Sew through to the next center (tack) bead and repeat around the cabochon.

Trimming and finishing
9. Very carefully trim your piece, leaving about a 1/16-in. (2mm) border so you don't trim the tack threads (**d**).

10. You are ready to glue your piece to the box. Using tacky glue and a tooth-pick, spread the glue onto the back of your piece, making sure to glue close to the edges (**e**).

11. Center the beadwork, glue side down, on the lid and press it into place. Use a cotton swab to clean up the excess glue and also to help press the finished piece onto the box lid (**f**).

Save those small lengths of thread for beading around small cabochons. Hang them on a tack near your desk.

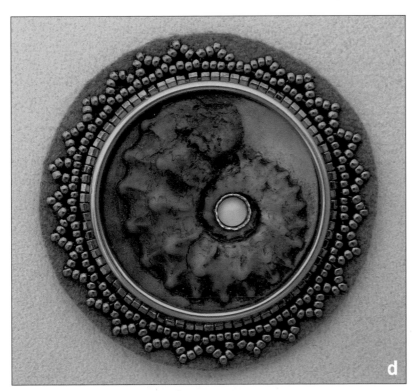

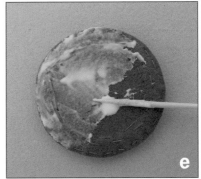

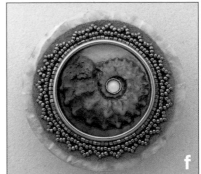

Heidi

We have all broken a beautiful piece of pottery or porcelain — something we cherished — and were reluctant to throw the pieces away. I'll show you how to make a pendant using one of those broken pieces — or perhaps you have some other found object you want to incorporate. Keep in mind, the item needs to be flat and not very thick. Also make sure that if the item is broken, as in porcelain or glass, you file or sand the sharp edges before using it.

Materials:
- Piece of porcelain or other found object, approx. 30 x 50mm
- Button, 1¼ in. (3.2cm) in diameter
- 10mm round cabochon
- 8 x 6mm cabochon
- 25 9º seed beads, brown iris
- 10g 15º seed beads, metallic gold
- V-neck choker blank, brass (Designer Findings)

Tools:
- Beading needle, #12
- Nymo B
- Toothpicks
- Scissors
- Fine-tip marker

Stitches:
- Backstitch 4, Backstitch 6, Webbing, Simple edging

Foundation, lining, and backing:
- Ultrasuede
- Lacy's Stiff Stuff

Adhesives:
- Two-part epoxy
- UFO glue
- Tacky glue

PORCELAIN PENDANT

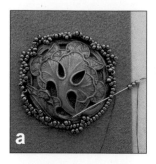

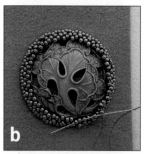

Planning your design

1. Find a button or metal stamping and cabochons that complement your porcelain. You can substitute a stone cabochon for the button — choose what flows with the piece and your personal taste.

2. Use beads and Ultrasuede that enhance the porcelain. Because the porcelain in this project has so much color, I chose to use only gold beads and let the porcelain and the stones be the focal point.

Gluing and stitching

3. Glue the button or the largest stone to the foundation using two-part epoxy. The button in this project was challenging because of its open front. I applied epoxy around the edge (but not in the center) so the open front of the button can be appreciated. Clean up any excess glue with a cotton swab and rubbing alcohol.

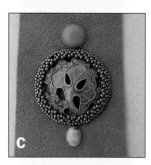

4. Single thread a #12 sharp needle with 1 yd. (.9m) of beading thread and tie a knot at one end. Push the needle up from the back of the foundation next to the button. Use 15º beads and backstitch 6 (see p. 22) around the button. Once this round is done, sew back through the beads again and then pull the round nice and snug against the button.

5. This project is a great example of design-as-you-go. Because the button's gluing surface is limited and the button edges are thin, it's best to work webbing (see p. 22) around the button to help hold it in place. Start the webbing by sewing up through one of the beads in the round. Pick up three 15º beads, skip three beads, and sew back out through the fourth bead. Continue around the button (**a**). After adding the first round of webbing, come up through the tack bead, pick up one 15º bead, and sew through the next tack bead. Continue around the button. Once you reach the starting point, pull the thread and snug the webbing up over the button (**b**).

6. Using UFO and a toothpick, glue the two cabochons to the foundation, applying pressure on the cabochons for 50 seconds for better bonding, and dry for 30 minutes before handling (**c**).

7. Using backstitch 6, stitch a round of 15º beads around each cabochon. On the 10mm cabochon, stitch a second round using the 9º beads and backstitch 6. For the small cabochon, use two 9º beads as accent beads on either side of the cab. Bead around the accent beads using the 15º beads and backstitch 4 (see p. 21).

8. Weave through the beadwork and exit a bead on the first round next to an accent bead. Work webbing as before, but this time sew through the beads again, tacking the center bead to the foundation (**d**). The webbing will be added only to the larger stone or button between the smaller cabochons. Once this is done, tie a knot on the back of your piece, and you're ready for trimming.

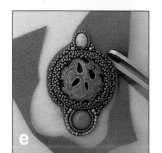

Trimming and finishing

9. Trim the excess Ultrasuede from the beadwork. Be careful as you trim so you don't cut the threads where you tacked the webbing to the foundation (**e**).

10. Once your piece is trimmed, you can glue it to the porcelain. Lay the finished beadwork on top of your porcelain and see where it looks the best. Using tacky glue and a toothpick, spread the glue on the back of the beadwork wherever it will come in contact

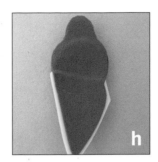
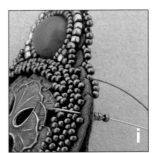

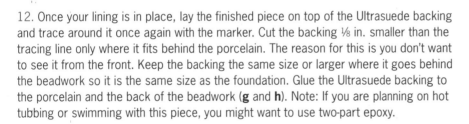

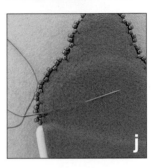

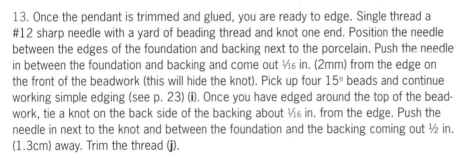

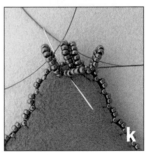

with the porcelain. Spread the glue out to the ends of the suede and press in place on the porcelain (**f**). Don't worry if the glue oozes out — this is easily cleaned up with a cotton swab and water. Use the cotton swab also to help push the foundation onto the porcelain.

11. Use Lacy's Stiff Stuff for your lining; the thickness of the Lacy's is great for this project because the porcelain is thick (you can use two layers if needed). Using a fine-tip marker, trace the top part of the beadwork onto the Lacy's. Cut the Lacy's ⅛ in. (3mm) smaller than the tracing line. Glue the lining to the back of the finished beadwork with tacky glue.

12. Once your lining is in place, lay the finished piece on top of the Ultrasuede backing and trace around it once again with the marker. Cut the backing ⅛ in. smaller than the tracing line only where it fits behind the porcelain. The reason for this is you don't want to see it from the front. Keep the backing the same size or larger where it goes behind the beadwork so it is the same size as the foundation. Glue the Ultrasuede backing to the porcelain and the back of the beadwork (**g** and **h**). Note: If you are planning on hot tubbing or swimming with this piece, you might want to use two-part epoxy.

13. Once the pendant is trimmed and glued, you are ready to edge. Single thread a #12 sharp needle with a yard of beading thread and knot one end. Position the needle between the edges of the foundation and backing next to the porcelain. Push the needle in between the foundation and backing and come out 1⁄16 in. (2mm) from the edge on the front of the beadwork (this will hide the knot). Pick up four 15º beads and continue working simple edging (see p. 23) (**i**). Once you have edged around the top of the bead-work, tie a knot on the back side of the backing about 1⁄16 in. from the edge. Push the needle in next to the knot and between the foundation and the backing coming out ½ in. (1.3cm) away. Trim the thread (**j**).

14. To make the bail, start a new thread with a #12 sharp needle and tie a knot at one end. Position the needle at the top center of the pendant between the foundation and backing to hide the knot, and come out the backing 1⁄16 in. from the edge. Pick up 15 15º beads or more, depending on your choker or cord size. Push the needle into the front of the foundation 1⁄16 in. from the edge and sew through to the back next to where you started. Repeat this process twice on each side of the first strand for a total of five strands, making a strong bail (**k**). You can change the number of beads and strands for your personal preference. You're ready to slide the pendant on your choker and wear it.

Heidi

I like to make lighter bracelets. A sterling cuff is a nice way to give a beaded bracelet an airy feeling. For this project, I chose pink aventurine, chrysocolla, and gaspeite, but I later changed the aventurine to amber as you can see in the photos. I encourage you to play with your own combination of stones and beads. Use what feels good to your soul. You can always change a stone if the color isn't working: Carefully push a flat metal ruler under the stone and slowly work around it to remove it. To adhere a new stone, use two-part epoxy or UFO glue. Don't spread the glue to the edges as you usually would. You don't want the excess glue getting onto your beadwork because it will be difficult to clean up.

Materials:
- 15mm cabochon
- 2 8 x 6mm cabochons
- 2 6mm cabochons
- Sterling cuff (Rio Grande)
- 10g 15° seed beads, metallic gold
- 100 9° seed beads, brown iris
- 1g Japanese cylinder beads, DB22
- 4 8° seed beads

Tools:
- #12 sharp needle
- Nymo B
- Toothpicks

- Clothespins
- Scissors
- Fine-tip marker

Stitches:
- Backstitch 6, Backstitch 4, Simple edging

Foundation, lining, and backing:
- Ultrasuede, poster board

Adhesives:
- Two-part epoxy
- UFO
- Tacky glue

STERLING CUFF BRACELET

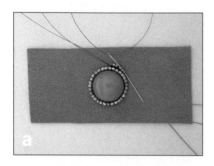

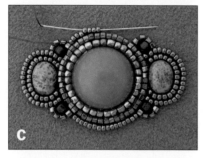

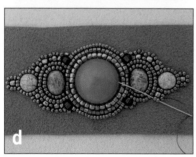

Planning the design

1. It's always good to lay out the button and stones you want to use ahead of time to see how they look together. This is also a good time to prepare any transparent cabochons by gluing them to foil as described on p. 27.

2. Select the color of Ultrasuede you will be using. Does it complement your stone selection? Make sure when you cut the suede you leave enough room for your beading and possible unplanned growth of your project. You never know what you might want to add after you've been beading for a while.

3. Choose your beads. I recommend using only three colors and/or sizes. Too many colors can confuse and clutter a design.

Gluing and stitching

4. Glue your cabochon in place using two-part epoxy (see adhesives p. 26). Set for at least 15 minutes before stitching.

5. For the first round of beads, use the 9ºs in gold iris. Using 1 yd. (.9m) of thread and a #12 sharp needle, tie a knot at one end. Bring the needle up next to the edge of the cabochon. Pick up six beads, and work backstitch 6 (see p. 22) around the cab or stone. You might have to adjust the number of beads picked up near the end of the round so they fit the shape of the stone. After you have connected the round, sew back through all the beads once again, pulling them nice and snug against the stone.

6. For the second round, position the needle next to the first round but not as close as you did to the stone, and work backstitch 6 using cylinders (**a**). Again, you might need to adjust the number of beads used toward the end. Sew through the second round of beads again, not pulling as snugly as before, but just enough to make them happy and sit nicely.

7. Glue the two matching cabochons next to the existing beads using UFO glue (be sure to sand the backs before gluing for added security) (**b**). If you've run short on thread, feel free to tie a knot on the back of the suede and add another yard of thread. Use 15º beads in metallic gold and backstitch for the next two rounds. Push the needle up from the back of the suede in next to the new cabochon where the existing beads meet and begin working the next two rounds. Remember to sew back through each round as before. After both sides have two rounds, add the accent beads. Use four 8ºs as the accent beads in the four corners where the two different beads meet. Simply stitch the accent beads in place. Make sure to go through the beads a couple of times to secure them. Use backstitch 4 (see p. 21) to stitch 9ºs around the accent beads. After these are done, add a round of 15ºs along the outside edge next to the cylinder beads. This visually pulls the piece together (**c**).

8. Glue the last two remaining cabochons in place as before. Make sure they are lined up or you might end up with a crooked bracelet. Using 15ºs and backstitch 6, embroider around the last two cabochons. Here again, add accent beads (this time use some 9ºs). Stitch two 9ºs on both ends and, using 15ºs and backstitch 4, bead around them. Repeat with the second cabochon (**d**). The additional accent beads make trimming the piece easier. If you have too many

nooks and crannies to cut around, it can be difficult, and then you also have to edge around them. These are just things to consider at this stage of the game.

Trimming and finishing

9. Now it's time to trim. Be careful here — you don't want to cut any threads (**e**). It's better to have too much suede than not enough. You need to leave enough suede for edging (in other words, something for your needle to grip).

10. Place your trimmed piece on poster board and trace around it using a fine-tip marker. Cut the poster board about ⅛ in. (3mm) smaller than the finished piece. With your thumb, give the poster board a nice curve; this will help your finished work glue nicely to the curve in the sterling bracelet. Glue the poster board to the back side of the beadwork. It's easier to apply the glue to the poster board than to the back of the beadwork. See how it gives the piece a nice curve?

11. Lay the finished beadwork with lining on your Ultrasuede backing and trace it with a fine-tip marker. Cut it out. Use a toothpick to apply tacky glue to the suede and adhere it to the middle inside of the sterling cuff. Put more tacky glue on the poster board (or lining), which is already glued to the back of the beadwork. Using a toothpick, carefully smooth it out to the edges and position the beadwork on top of the sterling cuff, aligning it with the suede backing. You did glue it in the middle, right? Use clothespins as clamps to hold the piece while the glue dries (**f**).

12. After your glue has dried for approximately 15 minutes, trim any additional suede backing that extends beyond the beadwork's trimmed edge. Single thread a #12 sharp needle with 1 yd. of beading thread and tie a knot at one end. Push the needle between the foundation and the backing, coming up through the front side of the foundation. Add four 15° beads and, using simple edging (see p. 23), edge your piece (**g**). You might need to increase or decrease the number of beads to navigate the corners. Once you're done with the edging, push the needle out through the back approximately $\frac{1}{16}$ in. from the edge, and knot. Then push the needle in close to your knot and under ½ in. of suede pulling the needle and thread through the suede. Trim your thread. You can easily clean up extra tacky glue with a cotton swab and water. Your masterpiece is done.

Picking up beads can be tricky. Try to hold your needle horizontally to your work surface so the beads won't roll back off the needle.

Heidi

You can find the most wonderful stones and fossils at Gem and Mineral shows, which are held all over the United States. This is where I found the trilobites used for these earrings. These amazing creatures became extinct about 245 million years ago. At Arey-sur-Cure in France, a 15,000-year-old human settlement, one of the artifacts found by archaeologists was a trilobite that had been drilled to be worn as an amulet. Fossils are great to use for jewelry because they have so much to share — you can feel the old energy becoming new again. Of course, if you don't happen to have a trilobite lying around, use what you have — maybe a stone you found in your yard. As long as it has a flat back, it's good to go.

Materials:
- 2 10mm cabochons
- 2 trilobites
- 2 8X6mm cabochons
- 10 charms, 5 per earring (polymer leaf charm by Klew, patina leaf from Fire Mountain Gems)
- 2 cylinder beads
- 4 6mm metal beads
- 32 3mm metal beads
- 8 2mm metal beads
- 6 8º seed beads
- 175 9º seed beads, dark brown iris
- 1 g Japanese cylinder beads, DB 22
- 1 g Japanese cylinder beads, DB 671
- 1 g Japanese cylinder beads, DB 783
- 10 g 15º seed beads, metallic gold
- 2 French-hook earring wires

Tools:
- #12 long and #12 sharp needles
- Nymo B
- Toothpicks
- Needlenose pliers
- Scissors
- Fine-tip marker

Stitches:
- Backstitch 4, Backstitch 6, Backstitch 8, Simple edging

Fringe:
- Straight fringe

Foundation, lining, and backing:
- Ultrasuede
- Poster board

Adhesives:
- Tacky glue
- Two-part epoxy

TRILOBITE EARRINGS

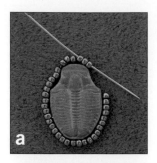

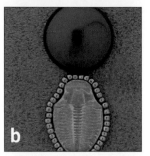

Planning the design

1. Lay out your stones to make sure they work well together and to determine the amount of Ultrasuede you need to cut for each earring. If you are using transparent stones, such as amethyst, now is a good time to glue these to aluminum foil (see p. 27). Also, if you are using black onyx, sand the back of the stone to ensure a good bond to the foundation.

2. Pick out the color of Ultrasuede you plan on using. Make sure it complements the stones. Additionally, use beads that complement your cabochon choices.

3. Find the charms you want to use for your earrings. Try to plan where you might place them — sometimes the longer ones work best in the middle.

Gluing and stitching

4. Begin by gluing the trilobite or the center stone in place. Use two-part epoxy and a toothpick to glue your stone, cleaning up any excess glue with a cotton swab and rubbing alcohol. Make sure that when you glue your stone to the Ultrasuede you allow room for your other stones. Let your glue set for 15 minutes before stitching any beads.

5. Single thread a #12 sharp needle with 1 yd. (.9m) of beading thread, and tie a knot at one end. Use 15º seed beads and backstitch 6 (see p. 22 and **a**) for round one. Accommodate any curve in the stone by using backstitch 4 (see p. 21) to fit the beads nicely in the curves.

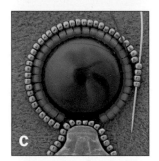

6. Glue the 10mm stone in place with two-part epoxy (**b**). Once the glue has set for 15 minutes, use Delica DB783s (or your choice of cylinder beads) and backstitch 6 to add a round of beads around the 10mm stone; don't forget to go back through the rounds to help pull them snug. For the second round, use 15ºs and backstitch 8 (see p. 22 and **c**).

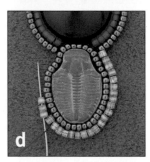

7. Begin the second round for the focal stone using Delica DB671s (or your choice of cylinder beads). Work backstitch 6; be sure to go back through the round when you are finished (**d**).

8. Glue the 8 x 6mm cabochon with two-part epoxy. Set the glue for 15 minutes before stitching. Use 2mm metal beads as accents: Stitch them to the foundation, going through them a few times. Stitch around the accent beads using 15ºs and backstitch 4 (**e**).

9. Work around the 8 x 6mm cabochon using 15ºs and backstitch 6. Sew the other two accent beads in place on both sides of the cabochon, and sew 15ºs using backstitch 4 to embroider around them. Finish by stitching 15ºs next to the cylinder beads around the center stone with backstitch 6. Then, stitch cylinders around the outside edge of the 10mm stone (**f**). Secure the thread as before, and trim.

10. Repeat steps 4–9 to make a second earring.

Trimming and finishing

11. Carefully trim around both finished pieces and trace them on poster board to get a lining pattern. Cut the traced pieces out about ⅛ in. (3mm) smaller than the actual size to keep the poster board from getting in the way of the edging. Glue the lining onto the back of the finished pieces using tacky glue and a toothpick. I find it easier to put the glue on the lining or poster board. Push the beadwork onto the lining so it's nice and flat and let it dry.

12. Now set the piece on the Ultrasuede backing and trace around it using a fine-tip marker. Cut the backing out. You are ready to glue the backing and foundation together using the

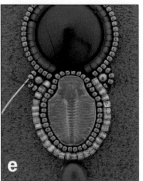

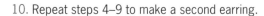

S'more technique (see p.28). If your earring findings have balls attached, cut them off with wire cutters. Bend the wire with needlenose pliers so it lies flat on the back of the earring lining. Use two-part epoxy to glue your earring wires, foundation, and backing together (**g**). Mix the glue with a toothpick and a piece of scrap paper. It's easier and cleaner to put the glue onto the foundation with the lining. Also, put some glue onto the loop of the ear wire. Position the cut backing in place. Dry the epoxy for 30 minutes before trimming so you don't get glue on your scissors. Once the glue dries, rubbing alcohol is the only thing that can remove it.

13. When the glue is dry, trim the excess backing. If you don't want to add fringe, you can use simple edging to finish your earrings. Or if you'd like fringe, continue to the next step.

Adding fringe

14. Measure the width of the bottom of the earring and cut a small piece of Ultrasuede to the measurement (**h**). It's best to cut it a little longer than needed. Use straight fringe (see p. 33). Use a fine-tip marker to put evenly spaced dots on the Ultrasuede where you want the fringe. This way you don't have to guess where to put the needle every time you start a new strand. Make sure to put the marks on the reverse side of the Ultrasuede so you won't see them once it's glued. Single thread a #12 long needle with 1 yd. of beading thread and tie a knot at one end. Push the needle into the back of the Ultrasuede at the first mark (again, this knot will be hidden once glued).

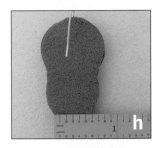

15. **Row 1**: Pick up 10 9ºs, three 3mms, three 15ºs, a charm, and three 15ºs. Skip the 15ºs and the charm, and go back up through the 3mms and the rest of the beads just strung. Continue adding fringe as follows: After stringing the bead sequence for each row, sew back through the last 3mms, the beads above, and the next mark on the Ultrasuede. Sew up through the front of the Ultrasuede at the next mark, pulling the beads in the fringe up to the bottom edge of the Ultrasuede. **Row 2**: 15 9ºs, a 3mm, an 8º, a 3mm, a cylinder, a 3mm, an 8º, a 3mm metal, and three 15ºs. **Row 3**: 20 9ºs, a 3mm, a 6mm, a 3mm, four DB671s, a charm, and four DB671s. **Row 4**: 10 9ºs, a 3mm, an 8º, a 3mm, 10 9ºs, five 15ºs, a charm, and five 15ºs (**i**). **Row 5**: 15 9ºs, three 3mms, three DB671s, a charm, and three cylinder beads. Go back up through the 3mm and the rest of the round. **Row 6**: 10 9ºs, a 3mm, a 6mm, a 3mm, four 15ºs, a charm, and four 15ºs. Go back up through the 3mm and the rest of the round. Push the needle through the back of the Ultrasuede, knot, and trim.

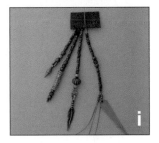

16. Glue the fringe strip to the back of the earrings using tacky glue and a toothpick. Put the glue onto the fringe's Ultrasuede, as you can work the glue into the knots (**j**). Dry the glue, then trim the excess Ultrasuede. Repeat with the second earring, sewing the fringe in the mirror image of the first.

Edging

17. Begin simple edging (see p. 23) at the top next to the wire. Single thread a #12 sharp needle with 1 yd. of thread and knot one end. Push the needle between the foundation and the backing, coming out through the front and hiding the knot. Pick up four 15ºs and push the needle in through the backing about ⅛ in. from the start. Come back out through the front and the fourth bead. Edge around the earring (**k**), increasing or decreasing the number of beads as you work to fit the earring's curves. When you reach the additional Ultrasuede from the fringe, stitch through it as though it were the backing. Carefully hold your fringe out of the way so you don't tangle the thread in it. Once you've edged all the way around the piece, go back through the first bead and tie a knot on the back. Push the needle in next to the knot and out about ½ in. away. Pull the thread through, and trim. Repeat with the second earring.

Heidi

Tree frogs and bird bones — if only we had some eye of newt, we could make a witch's brew. The tree frog by Laura Mears is sweet. I use her porcelain animals in many of my designs. This one is particularly nice because of the true size of the frog. The polymer clay bird bone adds a tribal feel, and the sage agate looks like water, as though the frog were looking at his reflection. I tried to use beads that would expand the water. Of course, this project is just an example of the possibilities. Find your own treasures and be creative in making your own brew.

Materials:
- Frog (by Laura Mears, Beyond Beads)
- Bird bone (Loco Lobo)
- Free-form cabochon (Gary Wilson)
- 1½-in. (3.8cm) pin back
- 15 1-in. (2.5cm) tube beads
- 64 4mm fire-polished beads
- 15 8° seed beads
- 15 3mm metal beads
- 5 g 15° seed beads, metallic gold
- 10 g 9° seed beads, brown iris
- 2 g cylinder beads, color to match stone

Tools:
- #12 sharp and long needles
- Nymo B
- Toothpicks
- Scissors
- Fine-tip marker
- Utility knife

Stitches:
- Backstitch 4, Backstitch 6, Backstitch 8, Simple edging

Foundation, lining, and backing:
- Ultrasuede
- Poster board

Fringe:
- Basic tube-and-crystal

Adhesives:
- Two-part epoxy
- Tacky glue

TREE FROG PIN

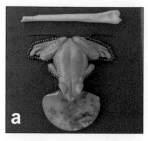

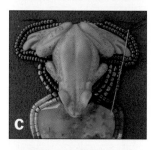

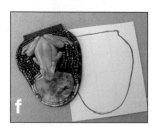

Planning your design

1. Select stones and colors that work well together, and be sure to cut enough foundation or suede to cover your design. Choose suede and beads that complement both your frog and stones. The only colored beads I used are ones that expand on the stone's natural beauty.

Gluing and stitching

2. Sand the back of the frog before gluing. As you glue your frog in place, position the stone and bone above and below to make sure you have enough suede to add them later. Use two-part epoxy to glue Mr. Frog. Look at his bottom and see where you will need to apply the glue (you are looking for any flat surface). Use a generous amount of glue. Once you have glued him down, clean up any excess glue with a cotton swab and rubbing alcohol, and allow the glue to dry for 15 minutes before stitching. This frog has a hole through him; use this to your advantage and stitch him down for added security.

3. Single thread a #12 sharp needle with 1 yd. (.9m) of beading thread and tie a knot at one end. Begin your first round of beads around the frog. Use 15°s and backstitch 4 and 6 (see pp. 21–22). You are using two different stitches because you have many curves to maneuver. Since you are going to be working the beads around, you might need to adjust the bead counts to make them fit. Place your bone next to Mr. Frog and mark the bottom of your bone with a fine-tip marker (**a**). These lines mark the boundary line for your beads, because the bone will be glued here in a later step.

4. Glue the free-form cabochon into place using the two-part epoxy and allow to dry for 15 minutes before stitching. Stitch the second round of 15°s around Mr. Frog using backstitch 4 and 6. Then start a round of beads around the cabochon using additional cylinder beads and backstitch 6. Try to extend the colors of the stone (**b**).

5. Stitch another row of beads next to the frog and around the cabochon using 9°s and backstitch 6. This is the last row around the cabochon. Continue adding rounds of beads on both sides of the frog, alternating the beads from 9°s to 15°s (**c**).

6. If you like the way this looks, you can stop and trim. I wanted to give my piece more texture, so I applied what I call the "anything goes" stitch. Adding anywhere from three to five beads at a time and varying the size, simply start stitching the beads to the foundation. There is really no right or wrong way to do this, except that you want the beads to continue in one direction so they flow together much like water flows down a stream (**d**).

Trimming and finishing

7. Trim the foundation, leaving a tab at the top for the bone (**e**). Trace the outline of the piece on poster board using a fine-tip marker (**f**). Cut the poster board ⅛ in. (3mm) smaller than the tracing lines and glue to the back of the foundation or finished beadwork using tacky glue. It's easiest to put the glue onto the lining and then press the lining onto the back of the beadwork. Make sure there are no clumps of glue or air pockets between the layers.

8. Lay the beadwork on the suede and trace the shape using the fine-tip marker. Cut the suede the same size or a little larger. On the reverse side, lay the pin back (in the opposite direction) and mark where the holes for the pin back need to be cut (**g**). Cut the holes with a utility knife. The reason you mark on the back of the suede is so you won't see the marks on the back of the finished piece.

9. Push the pin back through the holes so it is in the correct direction. Using a toothpick, mix

two-part epoxy on a piece of scrap paper. Apply the epoxy to the back side of the beadwork and between the Ultrasuede and the pin back for a good bond (**h**). Place the two back sides together. It's best to pick up the pin back from the side without glue and place it on top of the lining. If you do get any glue where you don't want it, clean up with rubbing alcohol. Allow the glue to dry for 30 minutes before trimming the excess backing.

10. Stitch the foundation and backing together along the top. Start on the left side of the tab and end on the right. Now you are ready to begin simple edging (see p. 23) (**i**).

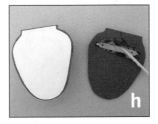

11. Once the edging is done, leave the thread attached and glue the bone into place using two-part epoxy. Put the glue onto the tab rather than the bone and allow it to dry for 15 minutes. You'll stitch beads around the bone to hold it in place and give the piece a primitive look. With the thread from the edging, push the needle into the backing at one end of the tab so it comes out behind the bone. Pick up 15 15º s (or more or less depending on the bone's size). Push the needle from the back to the front of your piece, next to the bone. Continue this process, adding and alternating the size and amount of beads and their placement. Make a second loop on the other end of the tab (**j**). When the loops are done, tie a knot on the back and push the needle next to the knot and out approx ½ in. (1.3cm) away. Trim the thread. If you want to add fringe, continue to the next step.

Adding fringe
12. Single thread a #12 long needle with 1 yd. of beading thread and knot one end. Use basic tube-and-crystal fringe (see p. 32), and always work from the reverse side so your fringe will be behind the edging. The edging will also work as a guide for spacing the fringe strands.

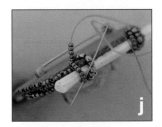

13. To determine where to start the first row, look at the piece from the front and push the needle in slightly on the right side of where you want the fringe to start. Turn the piece over and mark the spot with a pin. I like to work from left to right.

14. Push your needle in between the foundation and the backing, coming out the backing next to one of the sewn edge beads. **Row 1:** Pick up four 9ºs, a tube bead, two 9ºs, a 3mm, an 8º, a crystal, and five 15ºs. Skip the three 15ºs and sew back through the crystal and the rest of the beads just strung, and the front of the foundation, behind the edging, so the needle exits the backing where you started. Start the second row next to the first (approximately. ¹⁄₁₆ in.from the first) or next to the other edging bead. **Row 2:** Six 9ºs, a tube, two 9ºs, a 3mm, an 8º, two crystals, and five 15ºs. Skip the three 15ºs, go back up through the crystals and the rest of the beads in the row, and repeat as described before. Continue adding fringe. For each new row on the first half of the pin, pick up two extra 9ºs at the beginning of the strand and one extra crystal at the end. This will make your strand slightly longer each time.

15. When you reach the middle row, pick up 18 9ºs and eight crystals, then work the remaining fringe in the mirror image of the first half of the pin. Subtract two 9ºs and one crystal (**k**) with each new strand. To start a new thread (it takes a lot of thread to work this fringe), tie a knot on the back, push your needle in next to the knot and back out ½ in. away, and trim. Knot another thread and start as before, pushing the needle between the foundation and backing where you started. Continue edging and knot when complete (**l**). Use any type and number of beads for this fringe. Be creative. Create your own combinations. Use what works for you.

16. As a final touch, I added a little dangle in the front of my piece. This pulled the piece together by bringing the top embroidery into the fringe.

Heidi

Congratulations! You made it to the final project. By now you've learned the techniques and stitches and even discovered a few of your own. In this project, I'll teach animal embroidery (a turtle, the symbol for Mother Earth). Using Precious Metal Clay, I formed a fun shape using lizard hide for texture. And as you'll see from my first layout, some things have changed. I think this is important to know, because as you're stitching, you might realize that a certain stone or item may not be working with the design. Nothing is written in stone; go with your instincts … take a walk … breathe in the air … follow your heart.

Materials:
- 30mm vintage button
- 2 or 3 large cabochons of your choosing (Fossilized turtle shell and cabochons by Gary Wilson.)
- 2 matching cabochons for either side of the cuff
- PMC or similar metal stampings
- 4 x 6mm glass stone
- Brass necklace cuff (Designer Findings)
- 50g 15° seed beads, metallic gold
- 50g 15° seed beads, metallic silver
- 1g Japanese cylinder beads, black
- 1g Japanese cylinder beads, white
- 20 18° seed beads, black (for around turtle's eye)
- 1 hank 9° seed beads, brown iris
- 40 8° seed beads (for turtle shell)

Tools:
- #12 and #15 sharp needles
- Nymo B
- Toothpicks
- Pencil
- Fine-tip marker
- Poster board for pattern making
- Ruler
- Scissors

Stitches:
- Backstitch 4, Backstitch 6, Backstitch 8, Webbing, Snaking stitch, Simple edging

Foundation, lining, and backing:
- Ultrasuede
- Poster board or cereal box

Adhesives:
- Double-sided tape, two-part epoxy, tacky glue, UFO glue, rubber cement

ANCIENT SPIRALS COLLAR

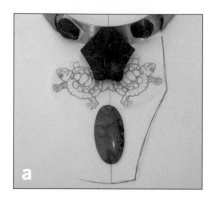

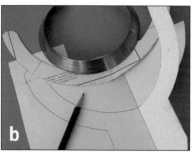

Planning the design

1. Lay out the stones on a piece of poster board with your cuff and use double-sided tape to place the items on the cuff to get an idea of how they will look (**a**). Copy the turtle pattern onto some tracing paper (I do this by taping the tracing paper onto a regular 8 x 11-in./20 x 28cm piece of paper and running it through the photocopier). You will need two turtles, unless you want more.

2. To get a pattern for your cuff, sacrifice a cuff and bend it flat. This will give you the exact size of the cuff. Make your pattern approximately ⅛ in. (3mm) larger than the actual cuff to allow for edging.

3. Once you have an idea of the stones' placement, lay them out on the poster board along with the cuff pattern. Make sure you have a center line so the collar will be symmetrical. Draw a line around your stones to get an idea of where you want the collar to end. Now you can cut out the pattern (**b**). Draw your shape on one half of the poster board, fold it in half and trace the other half. This way your pattern will be the same on both sides.

4. Trace around your pattern onto the Ultrasuede foundation (**c**). Make sure to transfer the center line as well (this well help in stone placement).

Gluing and stitching

5. Glue the center stone in place using two-part epoxy and let it dry. The center stone I used is a vintage button. Work backstitch 6 and backstitch 8 (see p. 22) to stitch around the button. The first round is with 9ºs and the second round is with metallic silver 15ºs.

6. Glue the next two stones in place. The large cabochon was sanded and glued with epoxy just below the button, and the turtle shell above. Because of the odd shape of the turtle shell, gluing was a challenge. I allowed for more room between the button and the shell. Because the shell is bent in the middle, I sanded the flattest side, and glued it down resting where the cuff will be (**d**). Use a row of 9ºs and work backstitch 6 around the turtle shell. Make sure the stones line up with the center line to keep the piece straight.

7. Work backstitch 6 and 8 to stitch around the large cabochon. The first round is 9ºs, the second round is 15ºs in metallic gold, and the third round is 9ºs. Add three- or five-bead webbing on the third round (see p. 22). Continue adding webbing and shaping the beads. Your webbing technique will become a snaking technique now; make it grow where you want it. Make sure to stitch a tack bead down every so often to keep the beadwork nice and flat. We'll come back later to add snaking beads (see p. 23).

8. Trim the turtle templates as closely to the edge as possible and glue them in place with the rubber cement (**e**).

9. Embroider the turtles' eyes first. It's always best to start with eyes no matter what animal you are creating. Use a black 9º for the eye. With 18ºs, a #15 needle, and backstitch 4 (see p. 21), go around the eye as shown (**f**). My hat's off to those of you who use the 18º beads — God bless you! Thank goodness we only need them for the eye detail! If they are just too small, you can get away with using 15ºs.

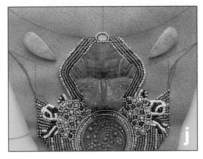

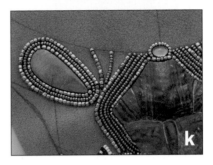

10. Using black and white cylinder beads, fill in the rest of the face and legs, working backstitch 4 and 6, so you have more control over the shaping and curves.

11. To make the turtles' shells, sew one 8º bead (color of your choice) along the edge of the shell. Add four to six 15º metallic silver beads and backstitch around the 8º bead. Add another 8º bead next to the 15º metallic silvers and continue around the shell, following the pattern as closely as possible until your shell is complete. You may need to add beads and make adjustments to accommodate your beads (**g**).

12. Repeat with the second turtle on other side (**h**).

13. Fill in the space between finished turtles and the webbing with 9º and 15º metallic gold beads, working in backstitch 6 and 8. Follow the curve of the button and then slowly fan out, staying within the lines of the pattern (**i**).

14. Sand the backs and then glue in the matching smaller cabochons (**j**). Notice a dotted line on the Ultrasuede. This is where you need to have flexibility so that the collar lays properly — so don't glue the stones here — make sure they are above or below the line. (The turtle shell has a natural bend in it, so I was able to get away with gluing it on this line.)

15. Once the glue is dry, stitch three rounds of beads around the stones. The first round is 9º s, the second is 15º metallic golds, and the third is 9º s (**k**). Fill in between the turtle shell and the matching stones as shown in (**l**). It's best to start a round of beads in the middle and then add arrows of beads in between.

16. At this point, go ahead and glue in the metal stamping or PMC components using UFO glue. I sanded the backs of the metal PMC for added security. Snug the metal stamping right up next to the beadwork already sewn. Add two rounds of beads, starting with 15º metallic golds and then 9º s. The beads naturally

As you design, consider flexibility where the cuff meets your collar bone. This shell has a natural curve, so it works nicely. You don't want to glue a stone here: either glue it above, to the cuff, or just below the cuff.

ANCIENT SPIRALS COLLAR

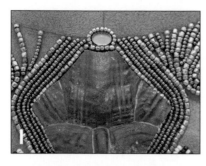

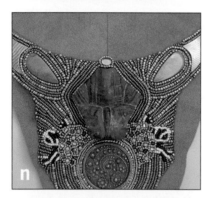

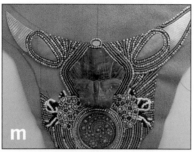

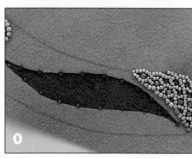

want to extend past the metal stamping and flow into the rest of the piece (**m**). You can now fill in between the turtle and the stones, sewing the beads in whatever direction you feel looks good (**n**). Try to keep your beads within the pattern that you have.

17. You can continue working all the way around the collar, if you wish. Make sure, again, that the beads stay within the pattern drawn on the Ultrasuede. I added some Ultrasuede patches for more color and a fun lining effect. To do this, first come up with a pattern on some poster board that fits into the space you have and flows with your piece. You also need to pick out suede or another material that will complement your design. You can use a number of things, such as ribbon, tapestry, or velvet. Once you have the pattern, trace around it on the backside of your collar with a fine-tip marker. (The reason you trace it on the back is so that if you don't cut it all away, you won't see the marker line.) Using a very sharp utility knife, cut out your pattern or shape. Cut the suede for the accent larger than the cut-out and use tacky glue to glue it into place. It's best to put the glue on the back side of your collar suede. This eliminates the guesswork in where to put the glue. Using a cotton swab and some water, clean up any excess glue. Use the swab to press the two pieces of suede together so they are nice and flat. You can use some beads to sew along the edge if you wish. This isn't necessary, but it looks nice and also helps secure the suede into place (**o**).

18. I added some snaking on the edge to help pull the piece together. Whenever you are webbing or snaking, you need to start with a round of beads (in this case 9°s worked well) and then add the webbing to the beads. You will have to adjust the number of beads so the snaking goes where you wish, then add the snaking beads in the holes. You are now ready to move on to trimming and finishing.

Trimming and finishing

19. Trim your piece using a good pair of scissors, following the pattern's line (**p**).

20. Using a firm lining (in this case some cardboard), trace behind the beadwork below where the cuff is. You don't need any lining where the collar rests, as this is stiff enough from the brass cuff. Glue the lining to the back of the finished beadwork using tacky glue. It is easier to spread the glue on the lining with a toothpick than on the back of the beadwork (**q**). Lay the piece on a flat surface and press the beadwork onto the lining, massaging it all over so it glues nice and flat.

21. Lay the piece on the backing and trace around it with a fine-tip marker (**r**). Cut out the backing. I find it's best to cut the backing where the cuff rests, right along the line. It's really hard to trim the excess backing off once the piece is glued into place. Now that you have cut out the backing, you can glue the finished beadwork to the cuff using tacky glue. For this project, it's best to apply the glue on the back side of the beadwork where the cuff will be glued (**s**). If you traced your pattern correctly, everything should glue right into place. At first it might seem that the beadwork is too small for the cuff. Stretch it out; it will cover the cuff, believe me. If you need to trim around the cuff so that the suede is symmetrical, now is a good time to do it. Next glue

the backing on using tacky glue. Put the glue on the brass cuff and lining. Once in place, trim any excess suede off, and you're ready for edging.

22. Edge your piece using simple edging (see p. 23).

23. If you're adding a drop (in this case a PMC drop), now is the time to do it. Since I glued an ammonite onto the front of the PMC, I also drilled holes in the PMC and sewed it in place as well for extra strength. I then adhered some suede to the back for a more polished look and also drilled holes on the top of the drop. If you are using another metal stamping, you will need to drill holes unless the stamping already has them.

24. Lay the stamping in place next to your collar to get an idea of how many beads you'll need to attach it, and where you want to start. Knot 1 yd. of thread with a #12 long needle on one end and push the needle between the foundation and the backing, coming out in the front of the foundation and edging where the first row will begin. I picked up 12 15º metallic gold beads to start my first row going in the front of the PMC stamping, and added 12 more 15º metallic gold beads and went into the backing directly in front of the first round. Push your needle through the suede and lining and come out on the opposite side. Do the same as before and make sure the drop is even. For the second row, you will have to add more or less beads, depending if it's on the outside or inside of the first round (t).

You're finished! Enjoy your beautiful collar.

TEMPLATE

Trace the turtle pattern directly, or photocopy it onto tracing paper by taping the tracing paper to copy paper and running it through the copier.

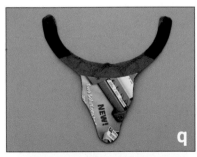

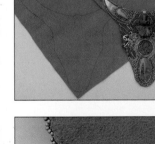

Feel of the Earth and the air;
be guided by good thoughts.
Absorb all that is around you.
Beauty is what you see and feel.
Let our creations spark you, but
create from your heart.

spiration

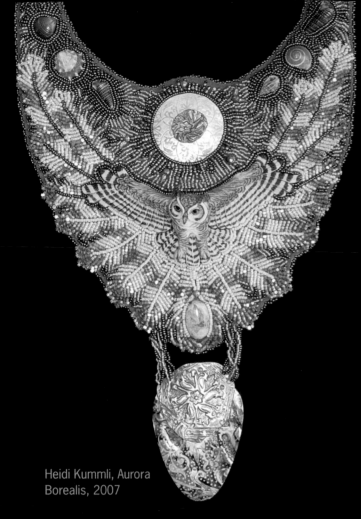

Heidi Kummli, Aurora
Borealis, 2007

Heidi Kummli, Puzzled
Prince, 2004

Heidi Kummli, Illusion, 2006

Sherry Serafini,
Genie's New
Hangout, 2006

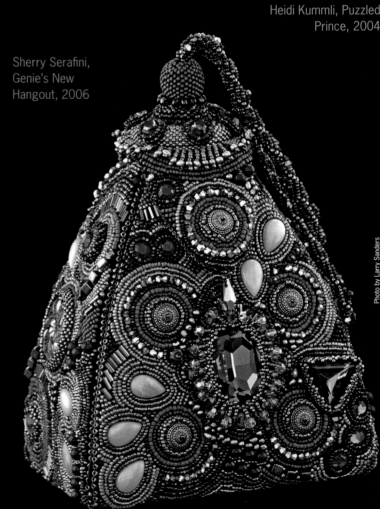

Sherry Serafini, Upstream, 2005

Heidi Kummli, Polar Melt Down, 2007

Sherry Serafini, Marley, 2006

Heidi Kummli, 2006

Sherry Serafini, Untitled, 2005

Sherry Serafini, Nicole, 2003

Heidi Kummli, June's Pin, 2006

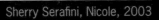

Inspiration **103**

Heidi Kummli, Dragonfly, 2006

Sherry Serafini, Untitled, 2004

Heidi Kummli, Ancient Forest, 2005

Sherry Serafini, My Dark Side, 2007

Sherry Serafini,
Mermaid's Attire, 2006

Sherry Serafini, The Queen's
Jewels, 2005

Sherry Serafini, Cuffs, 2003

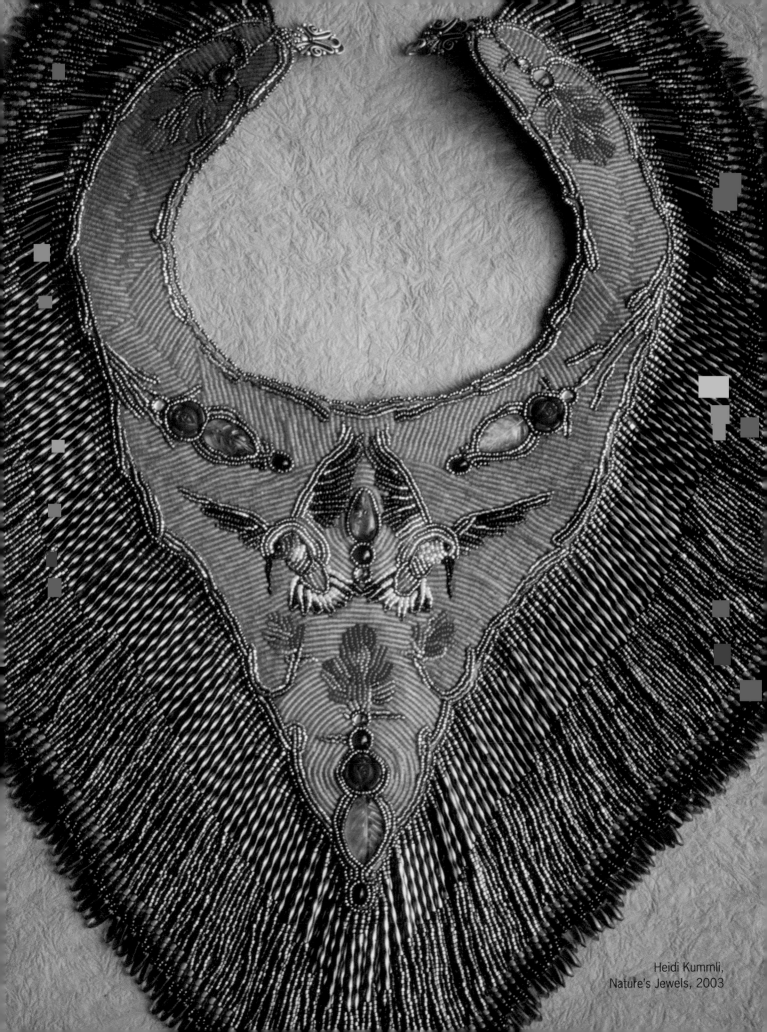

Heidi Kummli,
Nature's Jewels, 2003

Sherry Serafini, Million Dollar Baby, 2007

Heidi Kummli,
Pendant, 2002

Heidi Kummli, Imperial Jasper, 2002

Heidi Kummli, Native Spirit, 2007

Sherry Serafini,
Personal Journey.
2005

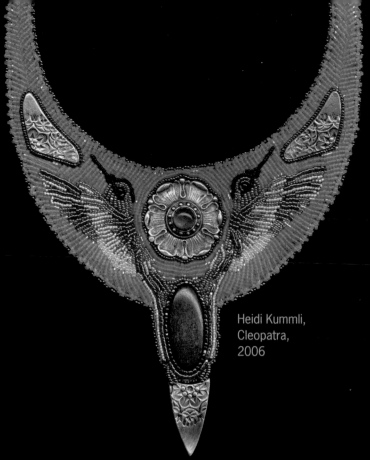

Heidi Kummli,
Cleopatra,
2006

Photo by Larry Sanders

Sherry Serafini, Dark
Side, 2006

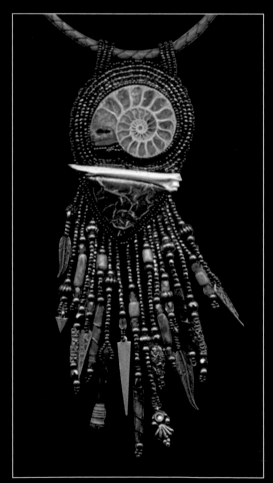

Heidi Kummli, Ammonite with Opal, 2001

Sherry Serafini,
Carnival, 2006

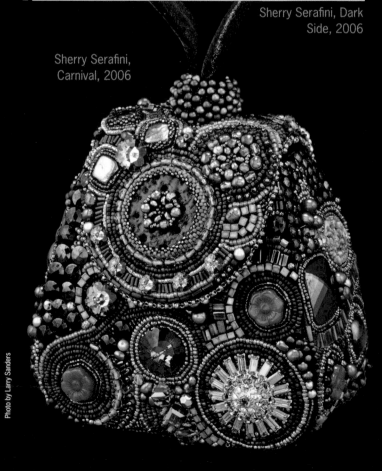

Photo by Larry Sanders

RESOURCES

Beads & Supplies

Beadcats
P.O. Box 2840
Wilsonville, Oregon 97070-2840
(503) 625-2323 fax (503) 625-4329
beadcats.com • orders@beadcats.com

Beyond Beadery
P.O. Box 460
Rollinsville, CO 80474
(800) 840-5548 fax: (866) FAX-BEAD
beyondbeadery.com
info@beyondbeadery.com

Fire Mountain Gems and Beads
One Fire Mountain Way
Grants Pass, OR 97526-2373
(800) 355-2137 fax: (800) 292-3473
firemountaingems.com

Ornamental Resources, Inc.
P.O. Box 3303/1427 Miner St.
Idaho Springs, CO 80452
(800) 876-6762
ornamentalresources.biz
orna@ornabead.com

Cabochons

Gary Wilson
garywilsonstones.com
sawrocks@aol.com

S&S Lapidary
P.O. Box 235
Sharps Chapel, TN 37866
(865) 278-3548
stunningstones.com

Findings & Silver

Designer Findings
P.O. Box 1433
Brookfield, WI 53008
(262) 574-1324 fax: (262) 547-8799
designersfindings.net
designersfindings@wi.rr.com

Nina Designs
P.O. Box 8127
Emeryville, CA 94662
(800) 336-NINA (6462)
ninadesigns.com
nina@ninadesigns.com

Rio Grande
7500 Bluewater Road NW
Albuquerque, NM 87121-1962
(800) 545-6566 • riogrande.com

Leather

Denver Fabrics
2777 W. Belleview Ave
Littleton, CO 80123
(866) 996-4573
denverfabrics.com
cs12@dfcustomerservice.com

Tandy Leather Company
3847 East Loop 920 South
Fort Worth, TX 76119
(800) 433-3201
www.tandyleather.com
leatherhelp@leatherfactory.com

Polymer Clay & Porcelain

Beyond Beads
12021 E. Sprague
Spokane, WA 99206
(509) 891-8653
beyondbeads.com • jodybead@aol.com

Earthenwood Studio
P.O. Box 20002
Ferndale, MI 48220
(248) 548-4793
earthenwoodstudio.com
earthenwood@comcast.net

Loco Lobo
5821 WCR 8E
Berthoud, CO 80513
(970) 532-3982
locolobodesigns.com
locolobo@earthlink.net

The Spirited Bead & Klews Designs
435 West J Street
Tehachapi, CA 93561
(661) 823-1930
klewexpressions.com
klew@klewexpressions.com

ACKNOWLEDGMENTS

Heidi Kummli • Free Spirit Collection
www.freespiritcollection.com
Thanks to everyone at Kalmbach Books for believing in our vision and actually making it come true. Thank you to my husband Gregg, and son, Ben, for their continued support and patience. Thanks to all our suppliers for their inspirational products and goodness. And thank you to my loving father who taught me the power of positive thinking and who always was excited to hear my dreams.

Sherry Serafini • Jewelry Design
www.serafinibeadedjewelry.com
Thanks to God from whom all gifts and talents are given. Greg, Erika, and Nikki for your support and patience with my sometimes out-of-control art! Mom and Dad, for giving me the courage to follow my dreams. My grandmother, for the inspiration she gave me since my childhood. My friends, who believed in me before I did, and encouraged me. My artist friend Ron Korczynski and his wife Judy for the incredible pottery (shown in the Design chapter). Our suppliers, who give both inspiration and true friendship. Our friends at Kalmbach for believing in us. Finally, my dear soul sister Heidi, whose beadwork has inspired me for years. Thanks for sharing this journey with me!

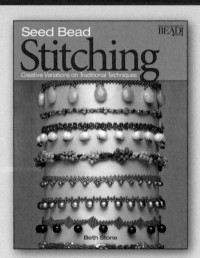